Calendar Collection

The Best and the Brightest in Calendar Design

Calendar Collection

Printed in Japan

P·I·E BOOKS
Villa Phoenix Suite 301, 4-14-6, Komagome, Toshima-ku
Tokyo 170-0003 Japan
Tel: 03-3940-8302 Fax: 03-3576-7361
e-mail: editor@piebooks.com sales@piebooks.com

ISBN4-89444-141-1

First Published in Germany 2001 by Nippan
Nippon Shuppan Hanbai Deutschland GmbH
Krefelder Strasse 85
D-40549 Düsseldorf Germany
Tel: 0211-5048080 Fax: 0211-5049326

ISBN 3-931884-78-3

本書は好評につき完売した「Calendar Graphics 2」の改訂版です。
This book was previously published in a popular hardcover edition as "Calendar Graphics 2."

CONTENTS

は　じ　め　に

　カレンダーをグラフィック・デザインの観点から捉えて早2冊目。本書をシリーズ化する
ほどのいきおいと、それに負けない収録作品の良さに、いかにカレンダーが人々の間で需要
が高いかを認識させられる。暦を読み取る、という本来の役目から日常の必需品となってい
るのか、市販品としても、企業の販促品としても、季節の節目が近づくと街をにぎわす代物
となる。

　どこがそんなに魅力的なのか ── 例えば企業のカレンダーの役割を考えてみると、半年、
長ければ1〜2年もの長期間消費者の生活に密着し、自社のプロモーション展開ができると
いう利点がまずある。企業広告といえば、ポスターやTVコマーシャルに代表されるような、
短期間限定でパッと花開き、消えていくというイメージが一般的だが、カレンダーならば、
ゆっくりと時間をかけて日々、月ごとに宣伝文句を伝えていくことができるのである。だか
らかもしれないが、本書に寄せられたもののなかでも、商品を具体的に勧めるカレンダーよ
りも、企業イメージが先攻する作品が非常に多い。自然をテーマにし、安らぎをイメージさ
せる会社や、スポーツを支援していることをアピールする会社、またページごとにデザイナ
ーやイラストレーターを変え、多方面の事業を強調している会社と、それぞれの戦略がペー
ジを繰るごとに楽しめるのである。どこか一方的な短期間限定広告よりも、暦が日常品だか
らか、結果的に消費者の歩幅でよみとるゆとりが感じられるのも、重要なポイントとなって
いるようだ。

　さてその一方で、昨今は内容がより簡素化されている傾向があるという話も、製作者側か
ら出ている。大判のものや絵柄が入ったものよりも、スケジュールが書き込める機能的な卓
上タイプのものがよく出回る、という。この原因を「不景気のせいでは」と評するひともい
るが、むしろ消費者の目が肥えてきたことを理由に挙げたい。オフィスやプライベート・ル
ームに置くものとして、より美しいものを望むのは自然なことだが、膨大な数のカレンダー
がそのつど生産される割に、それに見合ったものが数少なくなったという原因もあり得るの
ではないだろうか。それだけ日常の中でレベル高いデザインを求められているということは、
製作者側が再認識すべきことのように思うし、グラフィック・デザイン全般に言えることな
のだとも思う。

　前回のVol.1同様、本書でも世界各国のデザインが数多く一同に会しており、ページごと
カラフルに自己主張をしている。今後のより一層のグラフィック・デザイン向上のためにも、
本書がいい刺激剤になれば、と思っている。

ピエ・ブックス

FOREWORD

Here is a second volume looking at calendars from the viewpoint of graphic design. The remarkably high level of demand for calendars is evident from the brisk activity in calendar production that has warranted our bringing out a follow-up edition so quickly, and from the no less outstanding quality of artwork in the submissions we have received. Going beyond their original purpose of displaying the date, calendars have become a standard feature of our daily lives, and whether as products sold in shops, or as corporate promotional items given away to customers, they add to the atmosphere of intensifying activity as the end-of-year season approaches.

What is it that makes calendars so popular? From the standpoint of corporate enterprise, calendars first of all offer the advantage that they are admitted into the arena of consumers' daily lives for a comparatively long period of six months or even a year or two. Corporate advertising is generally thought of as something short-lived, appearing with a splash and disappearing almost immediately, as in the case of poster ads or TV commercials. But calendars can take their time and broadcast their message day after day over a period of weeks or months. Perhaps that explains why so many of the calendars submitted for the preparation of this book tend to plug corporate image rather than display any products or describe any services. Some companies want to conjure up an atmosphere of restful tranquillity by using features of the landscape, while others advertise the fact that they support certain sports. Still others use a different designer or illustrator for each page, perhaps to underline the diversified nature of their business. All these strategies can be readily appreciated by turning the pages of this book. In contrast to narrowly directed, limited term advertisements, it seems that what is considered important in promotional calendars is not pressurizing us with an acute sense of passing time, but encouraging us to feel that we are able to take life at our own speed.

On a different front, calendar producers have been pointing out a trend towards greater simplification in calendar design in recent years. They are saying that people these days no longer go for the large-size illustrated wall calendars. Rather it is the functional desk-top diary-type calendars in which appointments can be noted down that are becoming more common. There are some who attribute this to the recession, but we would like to suggest that one reason may be that consumers have become more discriminating. It's very natural to want something beautiful to display in one's office or home, but in reality, the enormous numbers of calendars produced precludes the possibility that many of them can come up to people's exacting standards. Could this not account for the changing trend? Calendar producers would do well to reappraise the high level of design that people have come to expect in all areas of their lives, and indeed this might be said for graphic design as a whole.

As in the first volume, this book features page after page of calendar designs brought together from countries all around the world, each colourfully claiming our attention. We at PIE Books hope that this book may serve to stimulate ever greater efforts towards high quality in graphic design.

P·I·E BOOKS

V O R W O R T

Hier ist der zweite Band, der Kalender aus der Graphik-Design-Perspektive betrachtet. Das bemerkenswert hohe Nachfrage-Niveau für Kalender ist an der forcierten Produktionsaktivität ablesbar. Das hat uns auch veranlaßt, diese Folge-Ausgabe von CALENDER GRAPHICS 1 so schnell zu veröffentlichen. Die Qualität der Einsendungen, die wir erhalten haben, ist weiterhin von hohem Standard. Kalender gehen heute über ihren eigentlichen Zweck, das Datum anzuzeigen, hinaus. Sie sind ein Teil unseres täglichen Lebens. Und ob als Produkt im Laden verkauft oder als Firmenwerbung an Kunden verschenkt, machen Sie einen Teil der Atmosphäre von intensiver Aktivität in der Jahresendphase aus.

Was macht Kalender so populär? Vom Standpunkt des Unternehmens bieten sie vor allem den Vorteil, daß sie im täglichen Umfeld des Kunden für eine verhältnismäßig lange Zeitspanne von meist einem Jahr geduldet sind. Firmenwerbung sieht man grundsätzlich sonst eher als kurzlebig. Sie tritt wie eine Welle auf und verschwindet auch bald wieder, wie im Falle von Plakaten oder Fernsehwerbung. Kalender dagegen können sich Zeit nehmen und ihre Werbebotschaft über Wochen und Monate senden. Das erklärt wahrscheinlich auch, warum so viele der uns gesandten Kalender eher das Firmenimage transportieren als Produkte zu zeigen oder Dienstleistungen zu beschreiben. Einige Firmen möchten eine Atmosphäre von friedlicher Stille vermitteln, indem sie Landschaftsmotive nutzen, während andere herausstellen, daß sie bestimmte Sportarten fördern. Wieder andere stellen auf jedem Blatt einen anderen Designer oder Illustrator vor, vielleicht um die Vielfalt des eigenen Geschäftes zu unterstreichen. Alle diese Strategien lassen sich leicht nachvollziehen, indem man in diesem Buch blättert. Im Kontrast zu eng begrenzten, kurzlebigen Anzeigen, scheint das Wichtige an Werbekalendern zu sein, uns nicht mit dem Eindruck der vorübergehenden Zeit zu bedrücken, sondern uns zu ermutigen, ein Gefühl zu entwickeln, daß wir in der Lage sind, die Geschwindigkeit unseres Lebens selbst zu bestimmen.

Kalenderproduzenten haben uns auch auf einen Trend zu größerer Einfachheit im Kalenderdesign der letzten Jahre hingewiesen. Sie sagen, daß Leute heute nicht mehr den großformatigen, illustrierten Kalender wollen. Es ist eher der funktionelle Schreibtischkalender, in den Termine eingetragen werden können, der heute verbreitet wird. Es gibt einige Leute, die dies der Rezession zuschreiben. Den Grund dafür sehen wir jedoch darin, daß Kunden wählerischer geworden sind. Es ist nur natürlich. daß jemand etwas für ihn Ansprechendes und Schönes in seinem Haus oder Büro aufhängt. Die große Zahl der tatsächlich produzierten Kalender schließt in der Realität aus, daß viele davon den Anforderungen der Leute entsprechen. Kann das auch einen neuen Trend bedeuten? Kalenderhersteller würden gut daran tun, den hohen Design-Standard wahrzunehmen, den die Leute heute in ihrem Lebensumfeld erwarten. Und in der Tat kann man das für das Graphik-Design als Ganzes behaupten.

Wie im ersten Band von CALENDER GRAPHICS präsentiert dieses Buch Seite für Seite Kalender-Designs aus aller Welt, jedes farbig nach unserer Aufmerksamkeit heischend. Wir von PIE Books hoffen, daß dieses Buch anregt, noch größere Anstrengungen hinsichtlich hoher Qualität im Graphik-Design zu unternehmen.

P·I·E BOOKS

Editorial Notes:

CD: Creative Director
AD: Art Director
D: Designer
P: Photographer
I: Illustrator
CW: Copywriter
DF: Design Firm

クレジットのタイトルは、クライアント名を表記しています。
また年度は使用年度を、国名は作品提供者の現住国を表記しています。

The credits are headed by the name of the commissioning client.
The year given is the year for which the calendar was issued.
The country indicated is the submittor's country of residence.

PHOTOGRAPHY

The Plantijn Group

Printing company / For promotional purposes   印刷 / プロモーション   Netherlands 1994
CD, D, P: Arno Bauman   D: Inge van Bremen / Emmy van Harskamp / Ivo van Leeuwen / Jan Pinto /
Inge van der Ploeg / Marco Stout / Indigo Klint Takeyama / Sylvia Suyker / Arjan ter Wiel
CW: Rien Vroegindeweij   DF: Studio Bauman bNO   size 560×480 mm

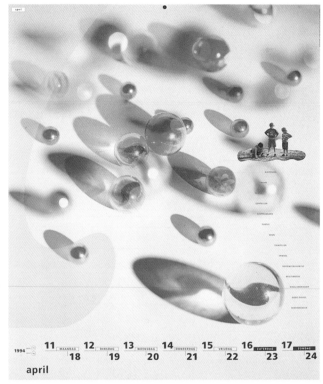

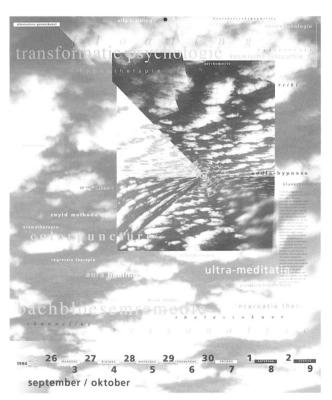

Guess?, Inc.

Apparel maker / For promotional purposes　アパレル メーカー / プロモーション　USA 1994
BR: Guess?, Guess? Jeans　CD, AD: Paul Marciano　D: Leslie Oki　P: Wayne Maser
DF: Guess? Advertising　size 335×455 mm

WED	THU	FRI	SAT
		1	2
6	7	8	9
13	14	15	16
20	21	22	23
27	28	29	30

MAY

SUN	MON	TUE	WED	THU	FRI	SAT
1	2	3	4	5	6	7
8	9	10	11	12	13	14
15	16	17	18	19	20	21
22	23	24	25	26	27	28
29	30	31				

DECEMBER

SUN	MON	TUE	WED	THU	FRI	SAT
				1	2	3
4	5	6	7	8	9	10
11	12	13	14	15	16	17
18	19	20	21	22	23	24
25	26	27	28	29	30	31

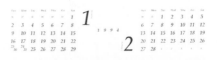
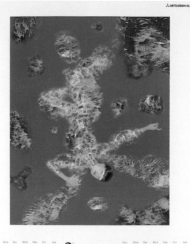

Mitsubishi Electric Corporation 三菱電機 ㈱

Electrical appliance manufacturer / For promotional purposes　電気機器メーカー / プロモーション
Japan　1993　1994　CD: Katsuhiro Miyawaki　AD, D: Tatsuhiko Fukazawa　P: Yukinori Tokoro
Planning: Ad. Melco　size 514×733 mm

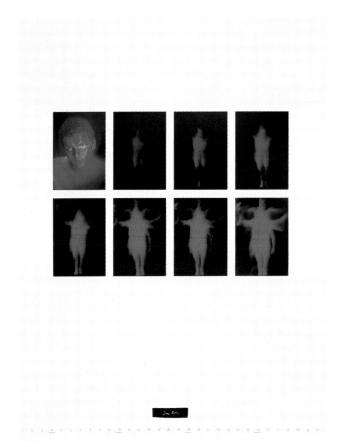

Kodak Foto Service

Photographic services / For promotional purposes　フォト サービス / プロモーション　Austria　1993
AD, D, I, CW: Sigi Ramoser　size 500×700 mm

**1995
CALENDAR**

MAURICE MARCIANO
PAUL MARCIANO
ARMAND MARCIANO

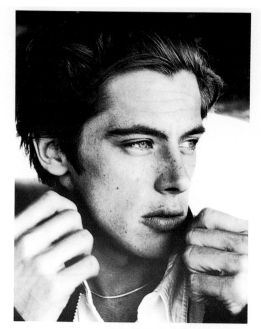

FEBRUARY

SUN	MON	TUE	WED	THU	FRI	SAT
			1	2	3	4
5	6	7	8	9	10	11
12	13	14	15	16	17	18
19	20	21	22	23	24	25
26	27	28				

SEPTEMBER

SUN	MON	TUE	WED	THU	FRI	SAT
					1	2
3	4	5	6	7	8	9
10	11	12	13	14	15	16
17	18	19	20	21	22	23
24	25	26	27	28	29	30

DECEMBER

SUN	MON	TUE	WED	THU	FRI	SAT
					1	2
3	4	5	6	7	8	9
10	11	12	13	14	15	16
17	18	19	20	21	22	23
24	25	26	27	28	29	30
31						

Guess?, Inc.

Apparel maker / For promotional purposes　アパレル メーカー / プロモーション　USA 1995
BR: Guess?　AD: Paul Marciano　D: Leslie Oki　P: Daniela Federici / Dewey Nicks　DF: Guess?, Inc.
size 340×460 mm

Studio No·ah Co., Ltd.　㈱ スタジオ ノア

Photographer / For promotional purposes
フォトグラフィー / プロモーション　Japan 1994
CD, AD, P: Hiroshi Nonami　D: Katsuyuki Tanaka
Hair, make-up & stylist: Yurika Uchida
size 300×300 mm

THE AMERICAN WEST: CULTURAL ENCOUNTERS, EXCHANGES & CELEBRATIONS

FOR CENTURIES, PEOPLE IN SPAIN PERFORMED THE MATACHINES DANCE. MOORISH IN ORIGIN, THE DANCE TRAVELED TO THE NEW WORLD AS PART OF THE CULTURE OF THE SPANISH COLONIZERS. INTRODUCED TO NEW MEXICO, THE DANCE PICKED UP INDIAN ELEMENTS, GESTURES AND MOTIFS. TODAY IT IS PERFORMED IN BOTH INDIAN PUEBLOS AND HISPANIC COMMUNITIES. THIS DANCE IS A GRAPHIC EXAMPLE OF THE MANY WAYS THAT DIFFERENT WESTERN GROUPS HAVE SHAPED AND ENRICHED EACH OTHER'S CUSTOMS. EACH PERFORMANCE IS, IN ITS ESSENCE A COLLABORATION BETWEEN THE PEOPLE OF THE DISTANT PAST AND THE PEOPLE OF THE PRESENT.

FEBRUARY						US WEST
Sunday	Monday	Tuesday	Wednesday	Thursday	Friday	Saturday
						1
2	3	4	5	6	7	8
9	10	11	12	13	14	15
16	17	18	19	20	21	22
23	24	25	26	27	28	29

THE AMERICAN WEST: CULTURAL ENCOUNTERS, EXCHANGES & CELEBRATIONS

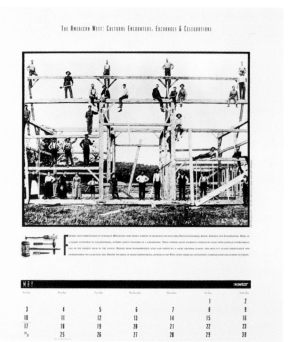

MAY						US WEST
Sunday	Monday	Tuesday	Wednesday	Thursday	Friday	Saturday
					1	2
3	4	5	6	7	8	9
10	11	12	13	14	15	16
17	18	19	20	21	22	23
24/31	25	26	27	28	29	30

THE AMERICAN WEST: CULTURAL ENCOUNTERS, EXCHANGES & CELEBRATIONS

JUNE						US WEST
Sunday	Monday	Tuesday	Wednesday	Thursday	Friday	Saturday
	1	2	3	4	5	6
7	8	9	10	11	12	13
14	15	16	17	18	19	20
21	22	23	24	25	26	27
28	29	30				

US West Communications

Telecommunications company / For promotional purposes   電信電話 / プロモーション   USA 1992
AD, D: Steve Wedeen   CW: Patricia Nelson Limerick / W. Clark Whitehorn
DF: Vaughn Wedeen Creative   size 460×405 mm

SUN	MON	TUE	WED	THU	FRI	SAT
·	·	1	2	3	4
5	6	7	8	9	10	11
12	13	14	15	16	17	18
19	20	21	22	23	24	25
26	27	28	29	30	31	·

1

SUN	MON	TUE	WED	THU	FRI	SAT
·	·	·	1	2
3	4	5	6	7	8	9
10	11	12	13	14	15	16
17	18	19	20	21	22	23
24/31	25	26	27	28	29	30

5

2

SUN	MON	TUE	WED	THU	FRI	SAT
·	·	·	·	·	·	1
2	3	4	5	6	7	8
9	10	11	12	13	14	15
16	17	18	19	20	21	22
23	24	25	26	27	28	29

6

SUN	MON	TUE	WED	THU	FRI	SAT
·	1	2	3	4	5	6
7	8	9	10	11	12	13
14	15	16	17	18	19	20
21	22	23	24	25	26	27
28	29	30	·	·	·	·

●● KOSÉ

●● KOSÉ

11

SUN	MON	TUE	WED	THU	FRI	SAT
1	2	3	4	5	6	7
8	9	10	11	12	13	14
15	16	17	18	19	20	21
22	23	24	25	26	27	28
29	30	·	·	·	·	·

7

SUN	MON	TUE	WED	THU	FRI	SAT
·	·	·	1	2	3	4
5	6	7	8	9	10	11
12	13	14	15	16	17	18
19	20	21	22	23	24	25
26	27	28	29	30	31	·

SUN	MON	TUE	WED	THU	FRI	SAT
·	·	·	·	·	·	1
2	3	4	5	6	7	8
9	10	11	12	13	14	15
16	17	18	19	20	21	22
23/30	24/31	25	26	27	28	29

8

SUN	MON	TUE	WED	THU	FRI	SAT
·	·	1	2	3	4	5
6	7	8	9	10	11	12
13	14	15	16	17	18	19
20	21	22	23	24	25	26
27	28	29	30	31	·	·

12

●● KOSÉ

●● KOSÉ

Kosé Corporation ㈱ コーセー

Cosmetics manufacturer / For promotional purposes　化粧品メーカー / プロモーション　Japan 1992
CD: Masuteru Aoba　AD, D: Michiko Sakurai　P: Jeanloup Sieff　CW: Tamotsu Kitahara
DF: Kosé Corporation, Advertising Dept.　size 595×420 mm

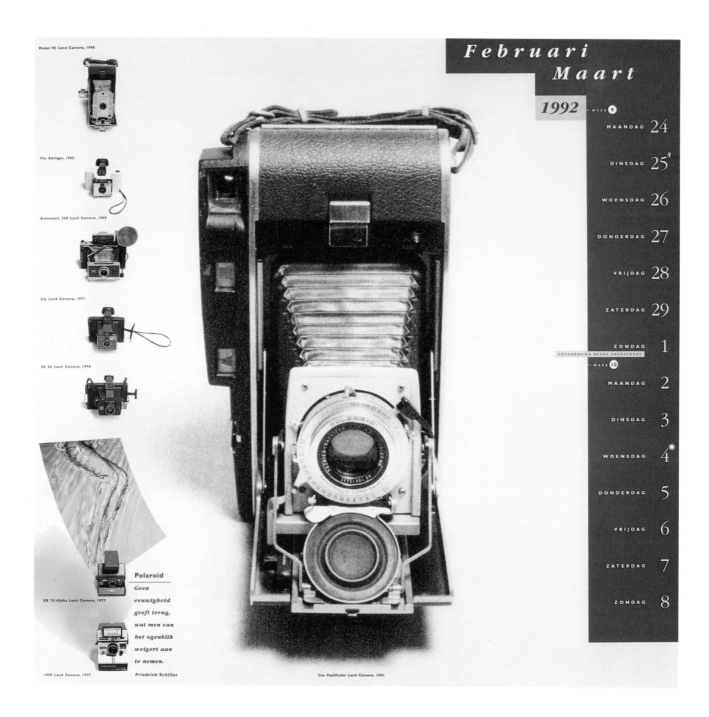

Model 95 Land Camera, 1948

The Swinger, 1965

Automatic 340 Land Camera, 1969

Zip Land Camera, 1971

EE 66 Land Camera, 1976

Polaroid

*Geen
eeuwigheid
geeft terug,
wat men van
het ogenblik
weigert aan
te nemen.*

SX 70 Alpha Land Camera, 1977

1000 Land Camera, 1977   Friedrich Schiller

The Pathfinder Land Camera, 1961

*Februari
Maart*

1992   week 9

MAANDAG 24
DINSDAG 25
WOENSDAG 26
DONDERDAG 27
VRIJDAG 28
ZATERDAG 29
ZONDAG 1
FOTOGRAFICA BEURS AMERSFOORT
week 10
MAANDAG 2
DINSDAG 3
WOENSDAG 4
DONDERDAG 5
VRIJDAG 6
ZATERDAG 7
ZONDAG 8

The Plantijn Group

Printing company / For promotional purposes　印刷 / プロモーション　Netherlands 1992
CD, D, P: Arno Bauman　CD, D: Emmy van Harskamp　D: Ivo van Leeuwen / Frans Pina / Jan Pinto /
Inge van der Ploeg　CW: Dr. Paul Hefting　DF: Studio Bauman bNO　size 480×480 mm

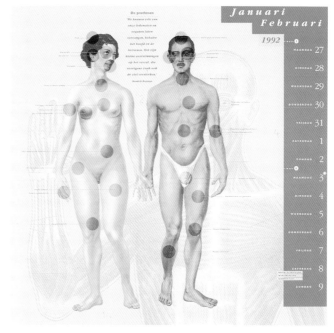

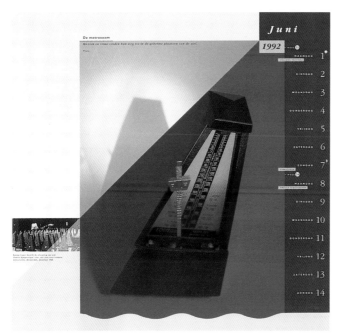

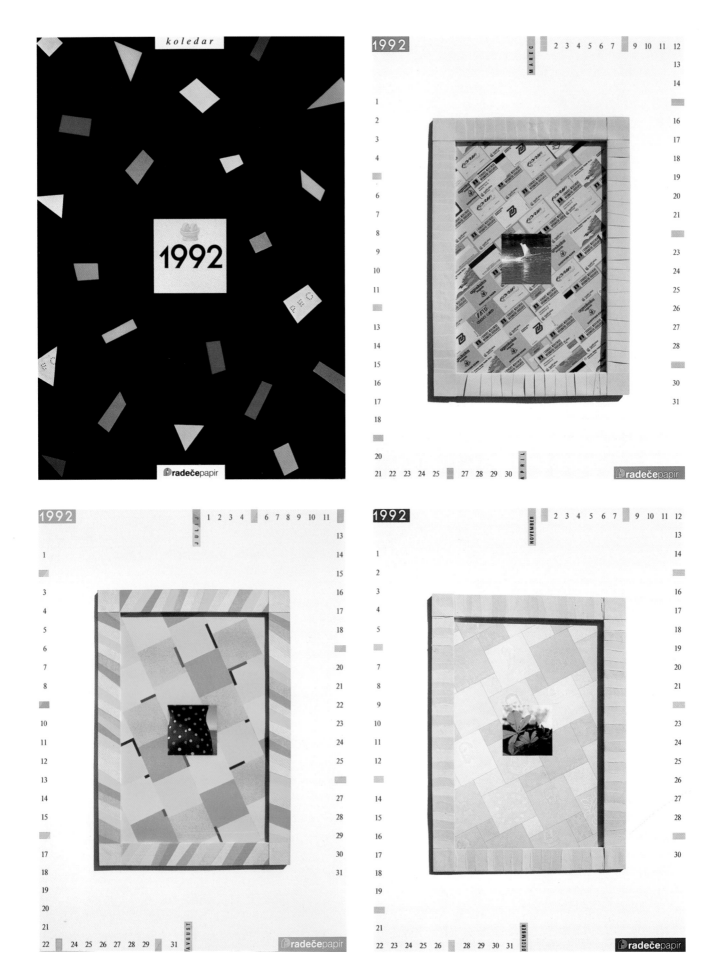

Radeče Papir

Paper manufacturer / For promotional purposes　製紙／プロモーション　Slovenia 1992
AD, D, I: Simon Sernec　P: Igor Knez / Marjan Dobovšek　I: Bojan Sumrak　size 675×480 mm

1992
Srečno novo leto
Happy New Year

Februar/February'92
1 2 3 4 5 6 7 8 9 10 11 12 13 14 15 16
17 18 19 20 21 22 23 24 25 26 27 28 29

Maj/May'92
1 2 3 4 5 6 7 8 9 10 11 12 13 14 15 16 17
18 19 20 21 22 23 24 25 26 27 28 29 30 31

Avgust/August'92
1 2 3 4 5 6 7 8 9 10 11 12 13 14 15 16 17
18 19 20 21 22 23 24 25 26 27 28 29 30 31

Krka

Pharmaceutical manufacturer / For promotional purposes   医薬品メーカー / プロモーション
Slovenia 1992   AD, D: Edi Berk   P: Dragan Arrigler   DF: Krog   size 380×580 mm

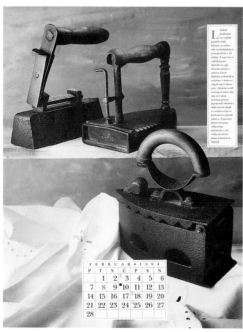

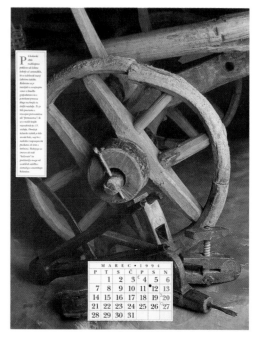

Kmečki Glas

Publisher / For promotional purposes　出版／プロモーション　Slovenia　1994
AD, D: Edi Berk　P: Janez Pukšič　DF: Krog　size 330×440 mm

Tiskarna Dan

Printing company / For promotional purposes　印刷／プロモーション　Slovenia　1993
AD, D: Edi Berk　P: Janez Pukšič　DF: Krog　size 380×580 mm

American President Lines

Shipping line / For promotional purposes　海運／プロモーション　USA 1993
AD, D: Jennifer Morla　D: Sharrie Brooks　P: Kathryn Kleinman　CW: Peterson Skolnick & Dodge
Stylist: Sara Slavin　DF: Morla Design　size 635×330 mm

❶

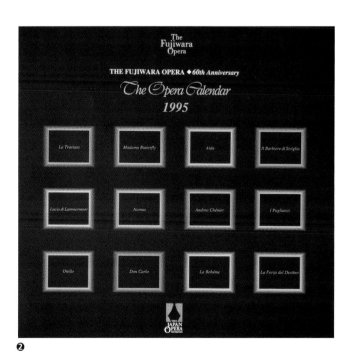

❷

❶
Leslie Evans Design Associates

Graphic design firm / For promotional purposes　グラフィック デザイン / プロモーション　USA　1994
CD, AD, D, P: Leslie Evans　D: Mary Brown　P: Jim Daniels　Stylist: Barbara Kurgan
size 480×760 mm

❷
The Japan Opera Foundation　日本オペラ振興会

Opera promoter / For promotional purposes　オペラ振興会 / プロモーション　Japan　1995
AD: Shinzo Honda　D: Masahiko Fuchikami / Noemi Oki　P: Masami Hotta　size 560×280 mm

	JULY 1991			AUGUST 1991		SEPTEMBER 1991

	OCTOBER 1991			NOVEMBER 1991		DECEMBER 1991

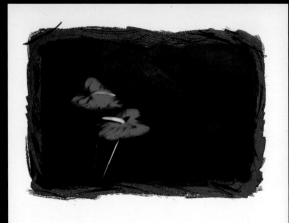

	APRIL 1991			MAY 1991		JUNE 1991

	JULY 1991			AUGUST 1991		SEPTEMBER 1991

Through the Lens Pty. Ltd.

Photographic services / For promotional purposes フォト サービス / プロモーション
Australia 1991 1992   AD, P: Peter Akbiyik   DF: Amanda Roach Design Pty. Ltd.
size 600×440 mm

1

Sun	Mon	Tue	Wed	Thu	Fri	Sat
					1	2
3	4	5	6	7	8	9
10	11	12	13	14	15	16
17	18	19	20	21	22	23
24	25	26	27	28	29	30
31						

NTTファシリティーズ

J a n uary

january

NTTファシリティーズ

june

Sun	Mon	Tue	Wed	Thu	Fri	Sat
		1	2	3	4	5
6	7	8	9	10	11	12
13	14	15	16	17	18	19
20	21	22	23	24	25	26
27	28	29	30			

6

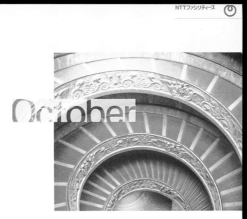

NTTファシリティーズ

September

Sun	Mon	Tue	Wed	Thu	Fri	Sat
			1	2	3	4
5	6	7	8	9	10	11
12	13	14	15	16	17	18
19	20	21	22	23	24	25
26	27	28	29	30		

9

October

10

Sun	Mon	Tue	Wed	Thu	Fri	Sat
					1	2
3	4	5	6	7	8	9
10	11	12	13	14	15	16
17	18	19	20	21	22	23
24	25	26	27	28	29	30
31						

NTT Facilities   NTT ファシリティーズ
Building design & management / For promotional purposes
ビル建築・運営・電力管理 / プロモーション   Japan 1993
CD, P: Fuyuki Fukada   AD, D: Haru Ishiwata   size 610×365 mm

Iwahashi Printing Co., Ltd. 岩橋印刷㈱

Printing company / For promotional purposes　印刷／プロモーション　Japan 1994
CD: Yukio Hikichi　AD, D: Ryohei Kudo　D: Mitsuhide Takahashi　P: Seiji Takihara
size 595×430 mm

Photographer Gou Tanabe, Art Director Yoshi Kishi, Kazuo Kogi, Sengou Morishita, Tatsuyuki Miura, Client Takesho Download: 37,200 2003

Photographer Gou Tanabe, Art Director Yoshi Kishi, Kazuo Kogi, Sengou Morishita, Tatsuyuki Miura, Client Takesho Download: 37,200 2003

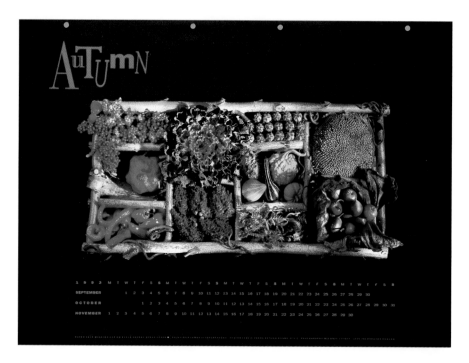

Leslie Evans Design Associates

Graphic design firm / For promotional purposes
グラフィック デザイン / プロモーション　USA　1993
CD, AD, D: Leslie Evans　D: Cheri Bryant　P: Michael Lisnet
Stylist: Barbara Kurgan　DF: Leslie Evans Design Associates
size 822×600 mm

Lek

Pharmaceutical manufacturer / For promotional purposes　医薬品メーカー / プロモーション
Slovenia　1990　AD, D: Edi Berk　P: Dragan Arrigler　DF: Krog　size 580×380 mm

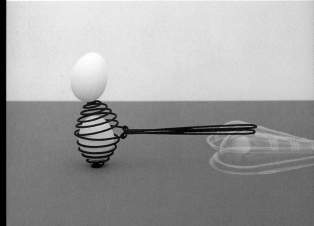

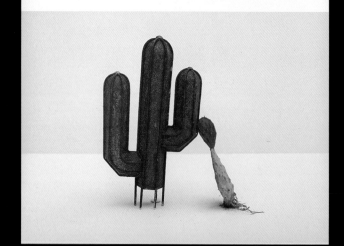

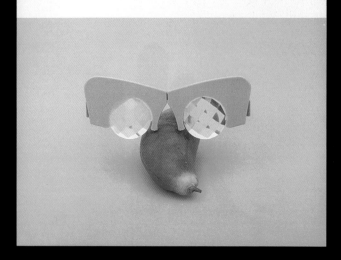

Hiroshi Yoda　与田弘志

Photographer / For promotional purposes　フォトグラフィー / プロモーション　Japan 1992
AD: Kazuya Mototani　D: Shinichiro Wada / Makoto Iida　P: Hiroshi Yoda　size 515×420 mm

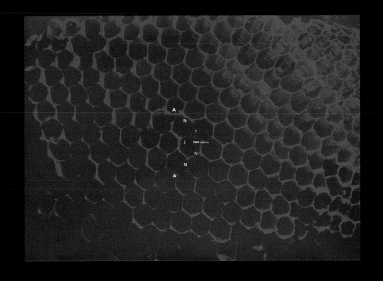

Beam ビーム

フォト スタジオ / プロモーション　Japan 1993

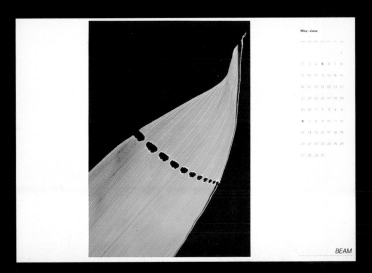

Beam ビーム

Photographic services / For promotional purposes
フォト スタジオ / プロモーション　Japan 1993
CD: Yukio Hikichi　AD: Ryohei Kudo　D: Mitsumasa Sugimoto
P: Seiji Takihara　size 600×425 mm

CALENDAR 1990
AESTHETIC
ANTHROPOMORPHISM

Designed by Masayoshi NAKAJO Photographed by Kichisaburo ANZAI

NTTデータ通信株式会社

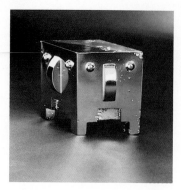

JANUARY	SUN	MON	TUE	WED	THU	FRI	SAT	1
		1	2	3	4	5	6	
	7	8	9	10	11	12	13	
	14	15	16	17	18	19	20	
	21	22	23	24	25	26	27	
	28	29	30	31				

FEBRUARY	SUN	MON	TUE	WED	THU	FRI	SAT	2
					1	2	3	
	4	5	6	7	8	9	10	
	11	12	13	14	15	16	17	
	18	19	20	21	22	23	24	
	25	26	27	28				

MAY	SUN	MON	TUE	WED	THU	FRI	SAT	5
			1	2	3	4	5	
	6	7	8	9	10	11	12	
	13	14	15	16	17	18	19	
	20	21	22	23	24	25	26	
	27	28	29	30	31			

JUNE	SUN	MON	TUE	WED	THU	FRI	SAT	6
						1	2	
	3	4	5	6	7	8	9	
	10	11	12	13	14	15	16	
	17	18	19	20	21	22	23	
	24	25	26	27	28	29	30	

SEPTEMBER	SUN	MON	TUE	WED	THU	FRI	SAT	9
							1	
	2	3	4	5	6	7	8	
	9	10	11	12	13	14	15	
	16	17	18	19	20	21	22	
	23 30	24	25	26	27	28	29	

OCTOBER	SUN	MON	TUE	WED	THU	FRI	SAT	10
		1	2	3	4	5	6	
	7	8	9	10	11	12	13	
	14	15	16	17	18	19	20	
	21	22	23	24	25	26	27	
	28	29	30	31				

NTT Data Communications Systems Corporation   NTTデータ通信㈱

Computer systems development, maintenance, sales, etc. / For promotional purposes
コンピュータ システム開発・保安・販売等 / プロモーション   Japan 1990
AD, D: Masayoshi Nakajo   P: Kichisaburo Anzai   size 730×510 mm

w t f s s m t w t f s s m t w t f s s m t w t f s s m t w t f
1 2 3 4 5 6 7 8 9 10 11 12 13 14 15 16 17 18 19 20 21 22 23 24 25 26 27 28 29 30 31

m t w t f s s m t w t f s s m t w t f s s m t w t f s s m t w t
1 2 3 4 5 6 7 8 9 10 11 12 13 14 15 16 17 18 19 20 21 22 23 24 25 26 27 28 29 30

11

Sony Corporation　ソニー ㈱

Audio-visual equipment maker / For promotional purposes
オーディオ ビジュアル機器 メーカー / プロモーション　Japan 1992
AD, D: Yoshie Nagasaka / Masayuki Kinoshita　P: Tadahisa Yoshikawa
DF: Sony Corporation, Corporate Design Center　size 445×530 mm

Ade S Publishing Inc. ㈱ アー ドゥ エス パブリシング

Publisher / For retail sales　出版／市販品　Japan 1995
CD, AD, D, P: Kijuro Yahagi　size 594×410 mm

Ade S Publishing Inc.　㈱ アー ドゥ エス パブリシング

Publisher / For retail sales　出版 / 市販品　Japan　1995
CD, AD, D, P: Kijuro Yahagi　size 594×410 mm

Honda Clio Kyoritsu Co., Ltd.　ホンダクリオ共立

Auto dealer / For promotional purposes
自動車ディーラー／プロモーション　Japan 1994
CD, CW: Kozo Koshimizu　AD: Setsue Shimizu　D: Koji Toda
P: Nobuo Nakamura　DF: HYPER + C'　size 425×590 mm

Kijuro
Yahagi

GALLERY
1995

KYOCERA　　　　CONTAX

January

1 2 3 4 5 6 7

8 9 10 11 12 13 14

15 16 17 18 19 20 21

22 23 24 25 26 27 28

29 30 31　　　　CONTAX

May

1 2 3 4 5 6

7 8 9 10 11 12 13

14 15 16 17 18 19 20

21 22 23 24 25 26 27

28 29 30 31　　　　CONTAX

March

1 2 3 4

5 6 7 8 9 10 11

12 13 14 15 16 17 18

19 20 21 22 23 24 25

26 27 28 29 30 31　　　　CONTAX

Kyocera Corporation　　京セラ ㈱ 光学機器事業本部

Optical instrument retailer / For retail sales　　光学機器メーカー / 市販品　　Japan　1995
BR: Contax　　size 780×475 mm

OCTOBER

SUN	MON	TUE	WED	THU	FRI	SAT
						1
2	3	4	5	6	7	8
9	10	11	12	13	14	15
16	17	18	19	20	21	22
23	24	25	26	27	28	29
30	31					

1994   **TIMEX**

APRIL

SUN	MON	TUE	WED	THU	FRI	SAT
					1	2
3	4	5	6	7	8	9
10	11	12	13	14	15	16
17	18	19	20	21	22	23
24	25	26	27	28	29	30

1994   **TIMEX**

DECEMBER

SUN	MON	TUE	WED	THU	FRI	SAT
				1	2	3
4	5	6	7	8	9	10
11	12	13	14	15	16	17
18	19	20	21	22	23	24
25	26	27	28	29	30	31

1994   **TIMEX**

Timex Corporation

Watch manufacturer / For promotional purposes 　腕時計メーカー / プロモーション 　USA　1994
CD, AD: Leslie Evans 　CD: Steve Treat 　AD, D: Mary Brown 　P: Stretch Tuemmler
DF: Leslie Evans Design Associates 　size 275×210 mm

*W*ith one edge of
our destiny established
on the shores of the oceans, we
staked out another at the edge of
the skies. It became tarmac and
technicians, glass and steel and
cement, passengers and pilots, cargo
and schedules in the wartime chaos
of 1944. The shriek of rubber as the
first plane touched down at our
new Seattle-Tacoma International
Airport sounded to some like the
sharp cry of an eagle laying claim
to a new domain.
In 1994 20,000,000 passengers
came and went at Sea-Tac—people
and cargo traversing a global
network of sea, air, rail and road.
So far the journey has taken over
80 years and touched on 350 countries. Fortunately we have a good
map for where we are headed
tomorrow.

JULY

S	M	T	W	T	F	S
						1
2	3	4	5	6	7	8
9	10	11	12	13	14	15
16	17	18	19	20	21	22
23	24	25	26	27	28	29
30	31					

AUGUST

S	M	T	W	T	F	S
		1	2	3	4	5
6	7	8	9	10	11	12
13	14	15	16	17	18	19
20	21	22	23	24	25	26
27	28	29	30	31		

1995

Port of Seattle

JANUARY

S	M	T	W	T	F	S
1	2	3	4	5	6	7
8	9	10	11	12	13	14
15	16	17	18	19	20	21
22	23	24	25	26	27	28
29	30	31				

FEBRUARY

S	M	T	W	T	F	S
			1	2	3	4
5	6	7	8	9	10	11
12	13	14	15	16	17	18
19	20	21	22	23	24	25
26	27	28				

1995

Port of Seattle

SEPTEMBER

S	M	T	W	T	F	S
					1	2
3	4	5	6	7	8	9
10	11	12	13	14	15	16
17	18	19	20	21	22	23
24	25	26	27	28	29	30

OCTOBER

S	M	T	W	T	F	S
1	2	3	4	5	6	7
8	9	10	11	12	13	14
15	16	17	18	19	20	21
22	23	24	25	26	27	28
29	30	31				

1995

Port of Seattle

Port of Seattle

Port authority / For promotional purposes　港湾整備・運営／プロモーション　USA　1995
CD: Margo Spellman　AD, D: Lynn Hernandez　D: Rick Way (Gage Design)　P: La Tona Productions
CW: Dick Patzke　DF: Port of Seattle　size 220×280 mm

JANUARY						睦月
Sunday	Monday	Tuesday	Wednesday	Thursday	Friday	Saturday
1	2	3	4	5	6	7
8	9	10	11	12	13	14
15	16	17	18	19	20	21
22	23	24	25	26	27	28
29	30	31				

FEBRUARY						如月
			1	2	3	4
5	6	7	8	9	10	11
12	13	14	15	16	17	18
19	20	21	22	23	24	25
26	27	28				

JULY						文月
Sunday	Monday	Tuesday	Wednesday	Thursday	Friday	Saturday
3	4	5	6	7	1	2
10	11	12	13	14	8	9
17	18	19	20	21	15	16
24 31	25	26	27	28	22	23
					29	30

AUGUST						葉月
7	8	9	10	11	5	6
14	15	16	17	18	12	13
21	22	23	24	25	19	20
28	29	30	31		26	27

Arai Construction Company　㈱ あらい建設

Construction company / For promotional purposes　建設 / プロモーション　Japan 1994 1995
CD, AD, D: Miyako Kimura　P, CW: Tadamichi Tanabe　DF: Design Office Eyespace
size 570×360 mm

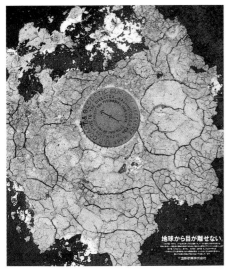

1992 Calendar

❶

May 5　　　June 6

September 9　　　October 10

❷

❶ Kokusai Kogyo Co., Ltd.　国際航業 ㈱

Global environment consultants / For promotional purposes
地球環境情報コンサルティング／プロモーション　Japan 1992
CD, AD: Osamu Takada　D: Kotoe Shindate　P: Hiroki Kitade
CW: Yuko Otsuka　DF: Takada Osamu Office　size 600×450 mm

❷ Fuji Megane　㈱ 富士メガネ

Eyewear retailer / For promotional purposes　眼鏡販売／プロモーション　Japan 1995
CD: Akio Kanai　AD: Hisao Sugiura　D: Masahiro Iwashige　P: Hiroki Kitade
DF: Studio Super Compass　size 370×255 mm

2 FEBRUARY   SUNDAY MONDAY TUESDAY WEDNESDAY THURSDAY FRIDAY SATURDAY   1 9 9 5

			1	2	3	4
5	6	7	8	9	10	11
12	13	14	15	16	17	18
19	20	21	22	23	24	25
26	27	28				

Canon

5 MAY   SUN MON TUE WEDNESDAY THURS FRI SAT   1995

	1	2	3	4	5	6
7	8	9	10	11	12	13
14	15	16	17	18	19	20
21	22	23	24	25	26	27
28	29	30	31			

Canon

11 NOVEMBER   SUNDAY MONDAY TUESDAY WEDNESDAY THURSDAY FRIDAY SATURDAY   1995

			1	2	3	4
5	6	7	8	9	10	11
12	13	14	15	16	17	18
19	20	21	22	23	24	25
26	27	28	29	30		

Canon

Canon Inc.　キヤノン㈱

Precision instrument supplier / For promotional purposes　精密機器製造・販売 / プロモーション　Japan 1995
AD: Kuniaki Soeda　D: Shu Gotoh　P: Kazuyoshi Nomachi　size 435×420 mm

Pentax Sales Company, Ltd.　ペンタックス販売 ㈱

Optical instrument retailer / For promotional purposes　光学機器 販売 / プロモーション　Japan 1995
CD, D: Mitsuo Katsui　P: Hideki Fujii　size 380×530 mm

OMRON

Omron Corporation　オムロン㈱

Electronic control equipment manufacturer / For promotional purposes
制御機器メーカー / プロモーション　Japan 1995
CD: Yoshimi Kobayashi　AD: Senshu Katsu　D: Kiyoshi Nakashima
CW: Tomoyuki Inoue　DF: CYBAC Co., Ltd.　size 600×420 mm

OMRON

1

SUNDAY	MONDAY	TUESDAY	WEDNESDAY	THURSDAY	FRIDAY	SATURDAY
1	2	3	4	5	6	7
8	9	10	11	12	13	14
15	16	17	18	19	20	21
22	23	24	25	26	27	28
29	30	31	1	2	3	4
5	6	7	8	9	10	11

OMRON

5

SUNDAY	MONDAY	TUESDAY	WEDNESDAY	THURSDAY	FRIDAY	SATURDAY
30	1	2	3	4	5	6
7	8	9	10	11	12	13
14	15	16	17	18	19	20
21	22	23	24	25	26	27
28	29	30	31	1	2	3
4	5	6	7	8	9	10

OMRON

8

SUNDAY	MONDAY	TUESDAY	WEDNESDAY	THURSDAY	FRIDAY	SATURDAY
30	31	1	2	3	4	5
6	7	8	9	10	11	12
13	14	15	16	17	18	19
20	21	22	23	24	25	26
27	28	29	30	31	1	2
3	4	5	6	7	8	9

MARCH 1995·3

JULY 1995·7

❶

2

FEB 1994

S	M	T	W	T	F	S
		1	2	3	4	5
6	7	8	9	10	11	12
13	14	15	16	17	18	19
20	21	22	23	24	25	26
27	28					

FUJI MEGANE

8

AUG 1994

S	M	T	W	T	F	S
	1	2	3	4	5	6
7	8	9	10	11	12	13
14	15	16	17	18	19	20
21	22	23	24	25	26	27
28	29	30	31			

FUJI MEGANE

❷

❶
Pioneer Electronic Corp.　パイオニア㈱

Audio-visual equipment maker / For promotional purposes
オーディオ ビジュアル機器 メーカー / プロモーション　Japan 1995
CD: Junichi Umehara　AD, D: Nobuo Suzuki　P: Umon Fukushima
size 420×594 mm

❷
Fuji Megane　㈱富士メガネ

Eyewear retailer / For promotional purposes　眼鏡販売 / プロモーション　Japan 1994
AD: Hisao Sugiura　D: Toshiro Matsuura　P: Hiroki Kitade　size 370×255 mm

明日、ラブレターを書こうと思う。

ホンダクリオ共立 東名川崎店 Tel.044-855-5611／中原店 Tel.044-755-1011／新横浜店 Tel.045-471-7901／港北ニュータウン店 Tel.045-942-4511／品川店 Tel.03-3450-1411／オートテラス Tel.045-473-7111

いつも、あなたを、おもっています。

ホンダクリオ共立 東名川崎店 Tel.044-855-5611／中原店 Tel.044-755-1011／新横浜店 Tel.045-471-7901／港北ニュータウン店 Tel.045-942-4511／品川店 Tel.03-3450-1411／オートテラス Tel.045-473-7111

いつも、あなたを、おもっています。

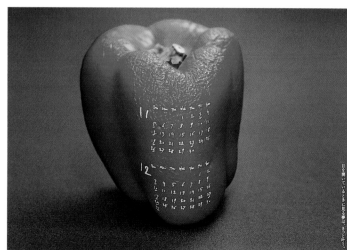

ホンダクリオ共立 東名川崎店 Tel.044-855-5611／中原店 Tel.044-755-1011／新横浜店 Tel.045-471-7901／港北ニュータウン店 Tel.045-942-4511／品川店 Tel.03-3450-1411／オートテラス Tel.045-473-7111

いつも、あなたを、おもっています。

Honda Clio Kyoritsu Co., Ltd.　ホンダクリオ共立

Auto dealer / For promotional purposes　自動車ディーラー／プロモーション　Japan 1995
CD, CW: Kozo Koshimizu　AD: Setsue Shimizu　D: Koji Toda　P: Hiroshi Harada　size 364×515 mm

THE FRUIT

New Oji Paper Calendar 1995

January 1 February 2

May 5 June 6

March 3 April 4

New Oji Paper　新王子製紙 ㈱

Paper manufacturer / For promotional purposes　製紙／プロモーション　Japan　1995
AD: Kazuya Takaoka　D: Tomoko Sugimoto　P: Sachiko Kuru　DF: DK Co., Ltd.　size 456×594 mm

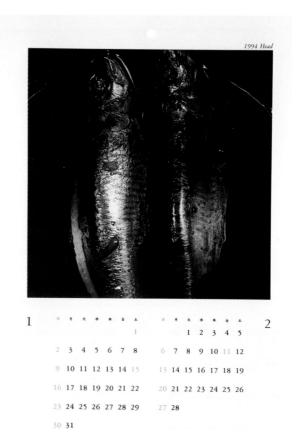

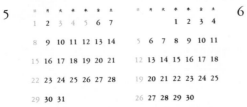

Head Co., Ltd. （有）ヘッド

Graphic design & advertising / For promotional purposes　広告制作 / プロモーション　Japan 1994
AD: Takeo Michinobu　D: Noriko Imamura　P: Tamotsu Fujii　CW: Kiyoshige Ogawa
size 320×230 mm

1

sunday	monday	tuesday	wednesday	thursday	friday	saturday
					1	2
3	4	5	6	7	8	9
10	11	12	13	14	15	16
17	18	19	20	21	22	23
24/31	25	26	27	28	29	30

2

sunday	monday	tuesday	wednesday	thursday	friday	saturday
	1	2	3	4	5	6
7	8	9	10	11	12	13
14	15	16	17	18	19	20
21	22	23	24	25	26	27
28						

6

sunday	monday	tuesday	wednesday	thursday	friday	saturday
			1	2	3	4	5
6	7	8	9	10	11	12
13	14	15	16	17	18	19
20	21	22	23	24	25	26
27	28	29	30			

10

sunday	monday	tuesday	wednesday	thursday	friday	saturday
					1	2
3	4	5	6	7	8	9
10	11	12	13	14	15	16
17	18	19	20	21	22	23
24/31	25	26	27	28	29	30

Art Print Japan Co., Ltd.　㈱ アートプリントジャパン

Stationery supplier / For retail sales　ポスター、カード製造・販売 / 市販品　Japan　1994
BR: graphic station　AD, P: Masao Yamamoto　D: Mutsuko Morita　size 400×260 mm

sunday	monday	tuesday	wednesday	thursday	friday	saturday	**1 2**	sunday	monday	tuesday	wednesday	thursday	friday	saturday
1	2	3	4	5	6	7	January February				1	2	3	4
8	9	10	11	12	13	14		5	6	7	8	9	10	11
15	16	17	18	19	20	21		12	13	14	15	16	17	18
22	23	24	25	26	27	28		19	20	21	22	23	24	25
29	30	31						26	27	28				

sunday	monday	tuesday	wednesday	thursday	friday	saturday	**5 6**	sunday	monday	tuesday	wednesday	thursday	friday	saturday
	1	2	3	4	5	6	May June					1	2	3
7	8	9	10	11	12	13		4	5	6	7	8	9	10
14	15	16	17	18	19	20		11	12	13	14	15	16	17
21	22	23	24	25	26	27		18	19	20	21	22	23	24
28	29	30	31					25	26	27	28	29	30	

sunday	monday	tuesday	wednesday	thursday	friday	saturday	**11 12**	sunday	monday	tuesday	wednesday	thursday	friday	saturday
			1	2	3	4	November December						1	2
5	6	7	8	9	10	11		3	4	5	6	7	8	9
12	13	14	15	16	17	18		10	11	12	13	14	15	16
19	20	21	22	23	24	25		17	18	19	20	21	22	23
26	27	28	29	30				24 31	25	26	27	28	29	30

Mitsubishi Motors Corporation   三菱自動車工業 ㈱

Auto maker / For promotional purposes   自動車メーカー / プロモーション   Japan 1995
CD: Takayuki Itoh   AD: Miwako Ebisawa   D: Hideko Hamanaka   P: Kaoru Ijima   CW: Kohji Sado
size 500×500 mm

September/September '92

1   2   3   4   5    7   8   9   10   11   12    14   15   16   17
18   19    21   22   23   24   25   26    28   29   30

July/July '92

1   2   3   4   5   6   7   8   9   10   11   12   13   14   15   16   17
18   19   20   21   22   23   24   25   26   27   28   29   30   31

Avgust/August '92

1   2   3   4   5   6   7   8   9   10   11   12   13   14   15   16   17
18   19   20   21   22   23   24   25   26   27   28   29   30   31

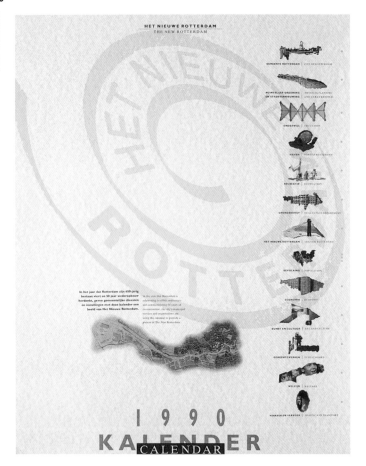

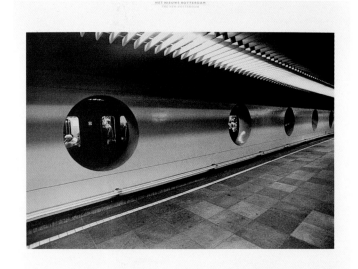

Gemeente Rotterdam (City of Rotterdam)

City public works department / For promotional purposes　ロッテルダム市 / プロモーション
Netherlands　1990　CD, D: Arno Bauman　D: Emmy van Harskamp / Jan Pinto
P: Daria Scagliola / Hans Werlemann / Chris de Jongh / Carel van Hees
CW: Information officers of municipal departments　DF: Studio Bauman bNO　size 630×490 mm

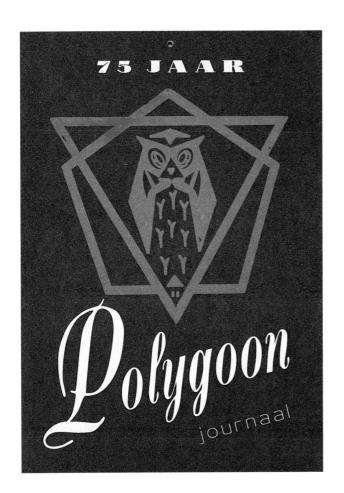

TEDDY SCHOLTEN

In maart 1959 wint Teddy Scholten het Eurovisie Songfestival.
Haar man Henk kust haar namens de hele Nederlandse bevolking.
March 1959: Dutch singer Teddy Scholten wins the Eurovision Song Festival.
Husband Henk gives her a kiss on behalf of the entire country.

ᵐ 03|09 ʷ
MARCH

MONDAY	TUESDAY	WEDNESDAY	THURSDAY	FRIDAY	SATURDAY	SUNDAY
28	01	02	03	04	05	06

DISTRIBUTION: NOS Sales ◆ ADDRESS: P.O. Box 26444   1202 JJ Hilversum   The Netherlands
TELEPHONE: (31)35 778037 ◆ TELEX 43470 ◆ TELEFAX: (31)35 775318

RAI

1948. Nederland heeft, 3 jaar na de oorlog, weer interesse voor nieuwe, luxe auto's,
zoals tentoongesteld op de RAI.
1948: Three years after the war, the Netherlands is once again showing interest in new luxury cars,
as can be seen at the RAI car fair.

ᵐ 06|23 ʷ
JUNE

MONDAY	TUESDAY	WEDNESDAY	THURSDAY	FRIDAY	SATURDAY	SUNDAY
06	07	08	09	10	11	12

DISTRIBUTION: NOS Sales ◆ ADDRESS: P.O. Box 26444   1202 JJ Hilversum   The Netherlands
TELEPHONE: (31)35 778037 ◆ TELEX 43470 ◆ TELEFAX: (31)35 775318

NIEUW GUINEA • NEW GUINEA

In december 1955 praten Nederland en Indonesië met elkaar over o.a. Nieuw Guinea.
De bevolking daar wordt bij deze besprekingen niet betrokken.
December 1955: The Netherlands and Indonesia hold talks concerning New Guinea.
The people of New Guinea are not involved in these talks.

ᵐ 12|50 ʷ
DECEMBER

MONDAY	TUESDAY	WEDNESDAY	THURSDAY	FRIDAY	SATURDAY	SUNDAY
12	13	14	15	16	17	18

DISTRIBUTION: NOS Sales ◆ ADDRESS: P.O. Box 26444   1202 JJ Hilversum   The Netherlands
TELEPHONE: (31)35 778037 ◆ TELEX 43470 ◆ TELEFAX: (31)35 775318

NOS

TV network / For promotional purposes   TV局／プロモーション   Netherlands 1993
CD, AD, D: Menno Landstra   DF: The Ambassadors of Aesthetics bv   size 220×155 mm

Aetna Corporate Affairs

Financial services / For promotional purposes　ファイナンシャル サービス / プロモーション
USA 1994   CD: Lisa Curran   AD, D: James Pettus   P: Anthony Barboza   I: Jim Coon
CW: Gary Frank   DF: Aetna Strategic Design   size 455×280 mm

口下手であがり性の 直属の上司

媒酌人は結婚退職では主義の直属の上司に結婚式のスピーチをお願いした。社会の厳しさや仕事のことを、一から教えてくれたやさしきこわい部長。私の経歴を詳しく書いているのに、書けば書くほど、その分、話が長くなると思うよね。愛想。披露宴の平均挨拶移動時間はなんと五分。それで締めくくる挨拶は、式場の担当者はほうの。「ありがたいお言葉は、すこし長めにいいのですよ」あのスピーチで、式場にも嫌われたら、かわいそうな部長。

あなたといっしょに考えたいから、…。
プラザヘイアン

「花嫁の父」にこだわる 花嫁の叔父

お父さんのすぐ下の弟。つまり私の叔父には、息子しかいない。近所にいるから小さい頃から、よく可愛がってくれた。時には、父親の役っている意味のコトを、やさしく他のコトで教えてくれた。「君のお父さんは、昔から、素直に言いだしたいとき、逆の言葉で言えないんだよ。本当は、嬉しいけど、淋しいんじゃないよ。」結婚式場でそんな話をしたら、「ありがとうのお花束を、叔父さんにもご用意致しましょうか」って、いってくれた。手間がかかることを平気で提案してくる。そんな願わしさがなぜか嬉しい。

あなたといっしょに考えたいから、…。
プラザヘイアン

JANUARY

SUN		MON		TUE		WED		THU		FRI		SAT	
26	先勝	27	先負	28	友引	29	先負	30	仏滅	31	大安	1	赤口
													元日
2	先勝	3	友引	4	先負	5	仏滅	6	大安	7	赤口	8	先勝
9	友引	10	先負	11	仏滅	12	赤口	13	先勝	14	友引	15	先勝
													成人の日
16	仏滅	17	大安	18	赤口	19	先勝	20	友引	21	先負	22	仏滅
23	大安	24	赤口	25	先勝	26	友引	27	先負	28	仏滅	29	大安
30	赤口	31	先勝										

APRIL

SUN		MON		TUE		WED		THU		FRI		SAT	
27	大安	28	赤口	29	先勝	30	友引	31	先負	1	仏滅	2	大安
3	赤口	4	先勝	5	友引	6	先負	7	仏滅	8	大安	9	赤口
10	先勝	11	友引	12	仏滅	13	大安	14	赤口	15	先勝	16	友引
17	先負	18	仏滅	19	大安	20	赤口	21	先勝	22	友引	23	先負
24	仏滅	25	大安	26	赤口	27	先勝	28	友引	29	先負	30	仏滅
										みどりの日			

私以上に張りきる 幹事さん

披露宴の式場が決まったら、次は披露宴の心配。自分の結婚式だからといって自分で司会をするというのもおかしな話。結婚式の受付からお願いまですべてを仕切らなければ気がすまない親友の弥生。未客が「さすが」と感じする若様を「ギ上の喜び」と感じている。やっとのことで進行案を持ってきた彼女。私の喜ぶ顔を見てニヤッと言えていた。「あなたの式場に行って、進行内容すべて決めちゃったよ」宴会場の人も親切だし、あなたに相談するの忘れてた。」だって

あなたといっしょに考えたいから、…。
プラザヘイアン

永遠のライバル、幼なじみ

幼稚園から高校まで同じクラスというのも、何かドラマチックなものを感じてしまう幼なじみ。小さいころから、私がひとつのことをやると必ず同じことをやって挑戦してくる。算数の家庭科、漢字のテスト、何から何まで、いつも競争していたみたい。久しぶりに電話して、結婚することを告げようとしたら、彼女から先に、「私、結婚するの」っていうの。驚いて、「まさか同じ式場だった。」「案の定、同じ式場を守れたら、式の日取りと相手が違うのが何よりも救って感じ。ふ！。

あなたといっしょに考えたいから、…。
プラザヘイアン

SEPTEMBER

SUN		MON		TUE		WED		THU		FRI		SAT	
28	仏滅	29	大安	30	赤口	31	先勝	1	友引	2	先負	3	仏滅
4	大安	5	赤口	6	友引	7	先負	8	仏滅	9	大安	10	赤口
11	先勝	12	友引	13	先負	14	仏滅	15	大安	16	赤口	17	先勝
								敬老の日					
18	友引	19	先勝	20	仏滅	21	大安	22	赤口	23	先勝	24	友引
										秋分の日			
25	先勝	26	仏滅	27	大安	28	赤口	29	先勝	30	友引	1	先負

DECEMBER

SUN		MON		TUE		WED		THU		FRI		SAT	
27	仏滅	28	大安	29	赤口	30	先勝	1	大安	2	先負	3	大安
4	赤口	5	先勝	6	友引	7	先負	8	仏滅	9	大安	10	赤口
11	先勝	12	友引	13	先負	14	仏滅	15	大安	16	赤口	17	先勝
18	友引	19	先勝	20	仏滅	21	大安	22	赤口	23	先勝	24	友引
								天皇誕生日					
25	先勝	26	仏滅	27	大安	28	赤口	29	先勝	30	友引	31	先勝

Heian Co., Ltd.　㈱へいあん

Bridal services / For promotional purposes　総合ブライダル事業 / プロモーション　Japan 1994
CD: Tac Amano　AD: Sunny Sanei　D: Hero Nishimura　P: Makoto Ikeda
CW: Etsu Saito　DF: White, Inc.　size 300×210 mm

❶

❷

❶
Honda Motor Co., Ltd.　本田技研工業 ㈱

Auto maker / For promotional purposes　自動車メーカー / プロモーション　Japan 1994
CD, AD, D: Hayato Kashiwagi　P: Tsuguo Tanabe, others　size 390×515 mm

❷
Honda Motor Co., Ltd.　本田技研工業 ㈱

Auto maker / For promotional purposes　自動車メーカー / プロモーション　Japan 1995
CD: Tadao Inaba　AD, D, CW: Yoshimi Kaneko　P: Haru Tajima　size 364×515 mm

DELEO CLAY TILE

❶

DELEO CLAY TILE

AS NATURAL AS THE PEOPLE WHO USE THEM

❷

❶
Deleo Clay Tile Co.

Tile manufacturer / For promotional purposes　タイル メーカー / プロモーション　USA 1990
CD, AD, D: Scott Mires　P: Chris Wimpey　DF: Mires Design, Inc.　size 600×910 mm

❷
Deleo Clay Tile Co.

Tile manufacturer / For promotional purposes　タイル メーカー / プロモーション　USA 1991
CD, AD, D: José Serrano　P: Chris Wimpey　DF: Mires Design, Inc.　size 540×910 mm

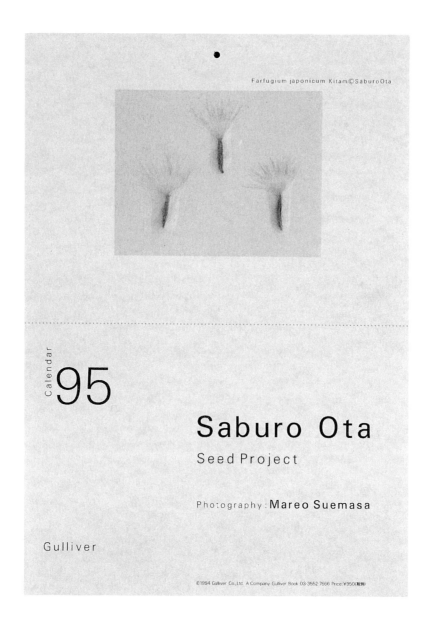

Farfugium japonicum Kitam©Saburo Ota

Calendar
95

Saburo Ota

Seed Project

Photography : Mareo Suemasa

Gulliver

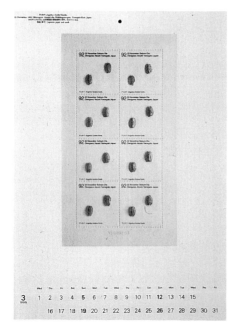

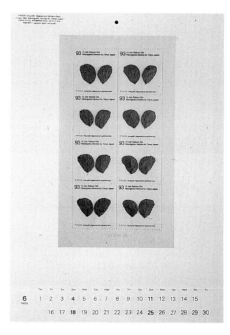

Gulliver Co., Ltd. ㈱ ガリバー

Printing company / For retail sales　印刷／市販品　Japan 1995　CD, Artist: Saburo Ota
AD, D: Tatsuomi Majima　P: Mareo Suemasa　DF: A Company Gulliver Book　size 257×182 mm

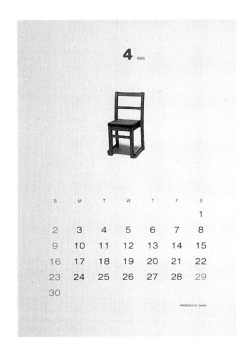

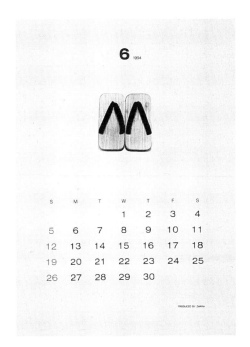

Zakka ザッカ

General merchandiser / For retail sales
雑貨販売 / 市販品　Japan 1994 1995
AD: Hitomi Yoshimura　D, P: Hiroki Kitade　size 274×200 mm

Kawai Steel　カワイスチール

Steel maker / For promotional purposes　鉄鋼／プロモーション　Japan 1992
AD: Fuyuki Fukada　D: Haru Ishiwata　P: Minoru Kobayashi　size 750×515 mm

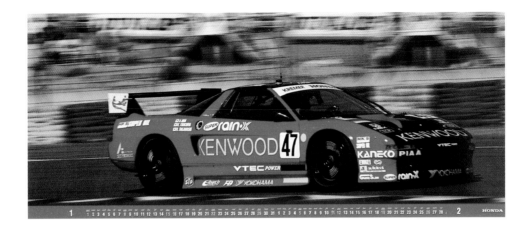

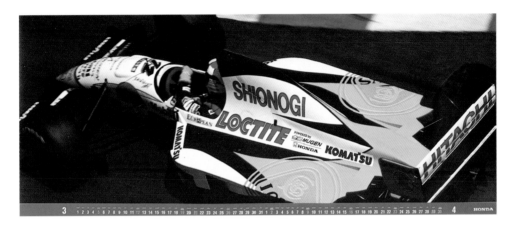

Honda Motor Co., Ltd.　本田技研工業 ㈱

Auto maker / For promotional purposes　自動車メーカー / プロモーション　Japan　1995
CD: Tadao Inaba　AD, D: Takeshi Nara　P: Fujio Hara　CW: Tsutomu Ishizaki　size 250×600 mm

february

1 2 3 4 | 5 6 | 7 8 9 10 11 | 12 13 | 14 15 16 17 18 | 19 20 | 21 22 23 24 25 | 26 27 | 28

the specials photographed by paul cox

march

1 2 3 4 | 5 6 | 7 8 9 10 11 | 12 13 | 14 15 16 17 18 | 19 20 21 22 23 | 24 25 | 26 27 | 28 29 30 31

april

1 2 3 | 4 5 6 7 8 | 9 10 | 11 | 12 13 14 15 | 16 17 | 18 19 20 21 22 | 23 24 | 25 26 27 28 29 | 30

Chrysalis Records

Record company / For promotional purposes　音楽ソフト メーカー / プロモーション　England　1994
CD, D: Wilf Whitty　　AD, D: Eddie Deighton　　P: Paul Cox / Nick Knight / Phil Knott
DF: Chrysalis Creative Dept. 'The Core'　size 420×297 mm

FEBRUARY

sun	mon	tue	wed	thu	fri	sat
		1	2	3	4	5
6	7	8	9	10	11	12
13	14	15	16	17	18	19
20	21	22	23	24	25	26
27	28					

JANUARY

OCTOBER

NTT ⏻

1995 NTT CALENDAR

SAE
ISSHIKI

NTT ⏻

1

1 2 3 4 5 6 7 8 9 10 11 12 13 14 15 16 17 18 19 20 21 22 23 24 25 26 27 28 29 30 31
Sun Mon Tue Wed Thu Fri Sat Sun Mon Tue Wed Thu Fri Sat Sun Mon Tue Wed Thu Fri Sat Sun Mon Tue Wed Thu Fri Sat Sun Mon Tue
• • • 1 2 3 4 5 6 7 8 9 10 11 12 13 14 15 16 17 18 19 20 21 22 23 24 25 26 27 28

2

NTT ⏻

5

1 2 3 4 5 6 7 8 9 10 11 12 13 14 15 16 17 18 19 20 21 22 23 24 25 26 27 28 29 30 31
Mon Tue Wed Thu Fri Sat Sun Mon Tue Wed Thu Fri Sat Sun Mon Tue Wed Thu Fri Sat Sun Mon Tue Wed Thu Fri Sat Sun Mon Tue Wed
• • • 1 2 3 4 5 6 7 8 9 10 11 12 13 14 15 16 17 18 19 20 21 22 23 24 25 26 27 28 29 30

6

NTT ⏻

7

1 2 3 4 5 6 7 8 9 10 11 12 13 14 15 16 17 18 19 20 21 22 23 24 25 26 27 28 29 30 31
Sat Sun Mon Tue Wed Thu Fri Sat Sun Mon Tue Wed Thu Fri Sat Sun Mon Tue Wed Thu Fri Sat Sun Mon Tue Wed Thu Fri Sat Sun Mon
• • • 1 2 3 4 5 6 7 8 9 10 11 12 13 14 15 16 17 18 19 20 21 22 23 24 25 26 27 28 29 30 31

8

Nippon Telegraph & Telephone Corporation　日本電信電話 ㈱

Telecommunications company / For promotional purposes　電信電話 / プロモーション　Japan　1995
AD, D: Fuyuki Fukada　P: Yoshinobu Aikawa　Model: Sae Isshiki　size 705×515 mm

Production Ogi ㈱ プロダクション尾木

Artist management / For retail sales　タレント プロダクション / 市販品　Japan 1994 1995
CD: Yoshio Tsutaki　AD, D, P: Aoi Tsutsumi　Model: Shizuka Kudoh　size 735×515 mm

Deleo Clay Tile Co.

Tile manufacturer / For promotional purposes　タイル メーカー / プロモーション　USA 1993
CD, AD, D: José Serrano　AD, D: Scott Mires　P: Chris Wimpey　DF: Mires Design, Inc.
size 840×430 mm

01
01 02 03 04 05 06 07 08 09 10 11 12 13 14 15 16 17 18 19 20 21 22 23 24 25 26 27 28 29 30 31 • •
TUE WED THU FRI SAT SUN MON TUE WED THU FRI SAT SUN MON TUE WED THU FRI SAT SUN MON TUE WED THU FRI SAT
01 02 03 04 05 06 07 08 09 10 11 12 13 14 15 16 17 18 19 20 21 22 23 24 25 26 27 28 • •
02

HIDEHARU SATOH

07
01 02 03 04 05 06 07 08 09 10 11 12 13 14 15 16 17 18 19 20 21 22 23 24 25 26 27 28 29 30 31 • • •
MON TUE WED THU FRI SAT SUN MON TUE WED THU FRI SAT SUN MON TUE WED THU FRI SAT SUN MON TUE WED THU FRI SAT
01 02 03 04 05 06 07 08 09 10 11 12 13 14 15 16 17 18 19 20 21 22 23 24 25 26 27 28 29 30 31
08

HIDEHARU SATOH

Hideharu Satoh Office　㈲ 佐藤秀春写真事務所

Photographer / For promotional purposes　フォトグラフィー / プロモーション　Japan 1991
AD, D: Motochika Ide　P: Hideharu Satoh　size 225×113 mm

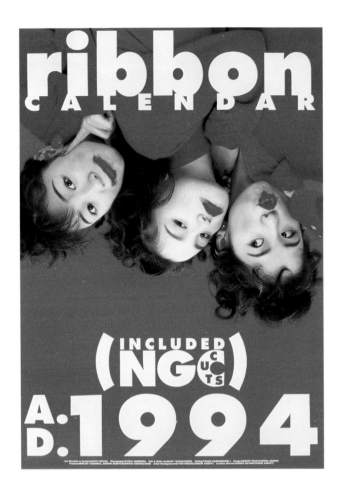

Tanabe Agency Co., Ltd.　㈱ 田辺エージェンシー

Artist management / For retail sales　タレント プロダクション/市販品　Japan 1994
CD: Kosuke Matsuo　AD: Kazuo Fukuda　D: Shigeru Okada　P: Ryuzo Minemura
Planner: Switch Corporation　Model: ribbon　size 520×360 mm

A–Images

Publisher / For retail sales　出版／市販品　USA　1993
CD, AD, D: Tin Yen　D, CW: Tommy Tam　P: Scott Hutchinson　CW: James Lee
DF: Mind's Eye Design　size 305×555 mm

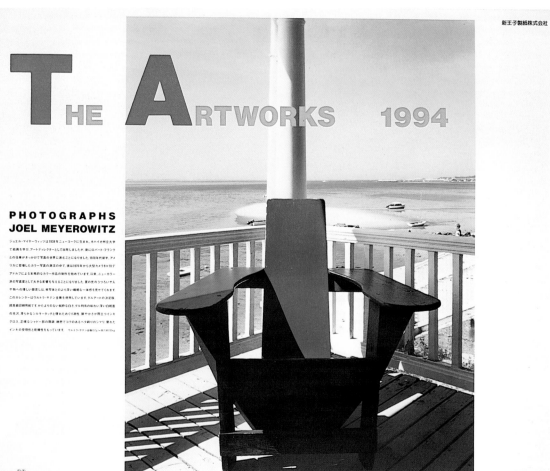

THE ARTWORKS 1994

新王子製紙株式会社

PHOTOGRAPHS
JOEL MEYEROWITZ

ジョエル・マイヤーウィッツは1938年ニューヨークに生まれ、オハイオ州立大学で絵画を学び、アートディレクターとして出発しましたが、後にロバート・フランクとの仕事がきっかけで写真の世界に進むことになりました。1970年代後半、アメリカに登場したカラー写真の源流の中で、彼は1976年から大型カメラ8×10でアドルフによる本格的なカラー作品の制作を始めています。以来、ニューカラー派の写真家として大きな影響を与えることになりました。夏の光のうつろいや人や物への優しい眼差しは、被写体とより深い機微を一体感を見せてくれます。このカレンダーはウルトラ・サテンを使用しています。ダルアートの決定版・超高級印刷用紙で、かたよりのない純粋な白さとダル特有の味わい深い紙面の光沢、滑らかなシルキータッチと優れためくり特性、鮮やかさが際立つラインマークロス、正確なシャドー部の再現、精密でコクのあるベタ刷りのシマリ、優れたインキの管理性と乾燥性をもっています。ウルトラ・サテン白122μ・四六判135kg

LOBSTER ROLL 3.25
CHEESEBURGER 1.25

New Oji Paper 新王子製紙㈱

Paper manufacturer / For promotional purposes 製紙／プロモーション Japan 1994
AD: Kazuya Takaoka   D: Tomoko Sugimoto   P: Joel Meyerowitz   DF: DK Co., Ltd.
size 515×620 mm

❶

❷

❶
Nippon Telegraph & Telephone Corporation　日本電信電話㈱

Telecommunications company / For promotional purposes　電信電話 / プロモーション　Japan 1991
AD: Fuyuki Fukada　D: Haru Ishiwata　P: Yoshihiko Ueda　Model: Hiroko Yakushimaru
size 670×515 mm

❷
Mizuno Corporation　ミズノ㈱

Sports equipment manufacturer / For promotional purposes
スポーツ用品製造・販売 / プロモーション　Japan 1995
size 515×728 mm

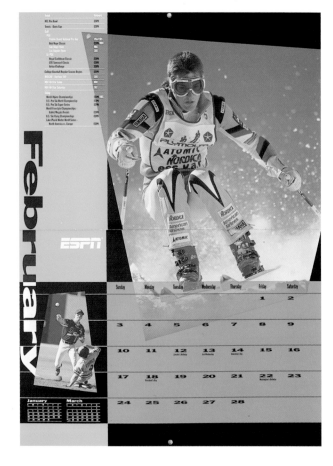

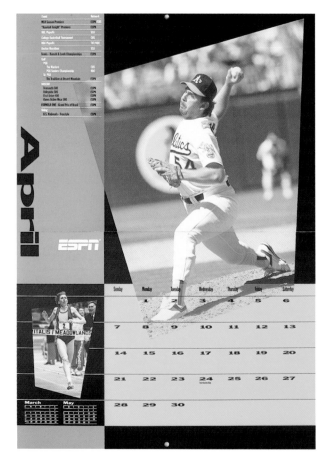

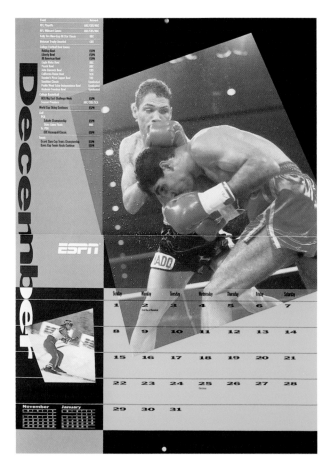

ESPN Inc.

Cable TV network / For promotional purposes　ケーブルTV局／プロモーション　USA 1991
CD, AD: Mark L. Handler　AD, D: Tom Dolle　D: Paul Biederman　CW: Howard Flashenburg
DF: Handler Group Inc.　size 600×430 mm

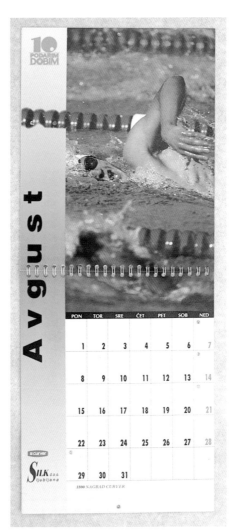

Podarim–Dobim

Sports promoter / For promotional purposes　スポーツ推進 / プロモーション　Slovenia 1994
CD: Ante Mahkota　AD, D: Simon Sernec　P: Joco Žnideršič / Aleš Fevžer / Zoran Vogrinčič /
Igor Modic　CW: Darko Vinkl　size 480×193 mm

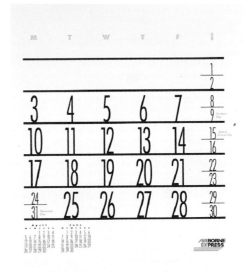

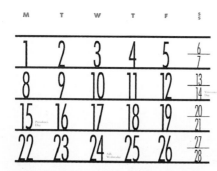

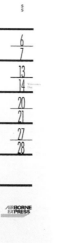

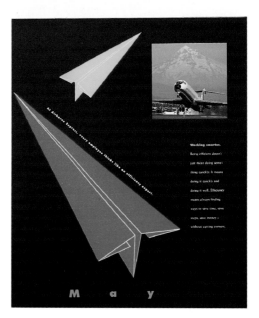

Airborne Express

Air courier / For promotional purposes　航空貨物サービス / プロモーション　USA 1993
AD, D: Julia Lapine　D: Heidi Hatlestad / John Anicker　DF: Hornall Anderson Design Works
size 610×250 mm

❶

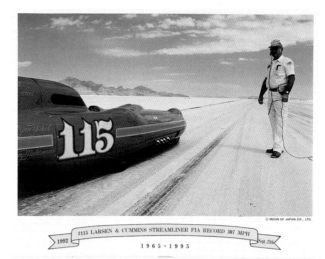

❷

❶ Moon of Japan Co., Ltd.   ムーン オブ ジャパン ㈱

Imported auto parts supplier / For promotional purposes
輸入オートパーツ、ノベルティ グッズ販売 / プロモーション   Japan 1995
BR: Mooneyes   size 440×280 mm

❷ Cadbury Beverages Canada Inc.

Beverage manufacturer / For promotional purposes   飲料メーカー / プロモーション   Canada 1994
D, I: Andy Ip   size 275×152 mm

On August, it's time for beachballs!

Spending quality time with your beachball is fun!

AUGUST

1994

se a proper inflation device.

PRINTING CONTROL

M1
T2
W3
T4
F5
S6
S7
M8
T9
W10
T11
F12
S13
S14
M15
T16
W17
T18
F19
S
M22
T23
W24
T25
F26
S27
S28
M29
T30
W31

Printing Control

Printing company / For promotional purposes
印刷 / プロモーション   USA 1994   D: Robert M. Brunz

Good health begins with you. And with a balanced diet, the proper nourishment and regular exercise, it can blossom.

1	T
2	W
3	T
4	F
5	S
6	M
7	T
8	W
9	T
10	F
11	
12	
13	S
14	M
15	T
16	W
17	T
18	F
19	
20	
21	M
22	T
23	W
24	T
25	F
26	S
27	
28	M

Eating fruits, vegetables and grains can help you lose weight permanently and prevent future health problems.

INOVA HEALTH SYSTEM — *February*

There are few things more valuable than knowing how the air in your lungs can breathe life into someone else.

1	M
2	T
3	W
4	T
5	F
6	S
7	S
8	M
9	T
10	W
11	T
12	F
13	S
14	S
15	M
16	T
17	W
18	T
19	F
20	S
21	S
22	M
23	T
24	W
25	T
26	F
27	S
28	S
29	M
30	T
31	W

Learn lifesaving CPR from Inova: Project CPR classes. To register, call Inova HealthSource at 703-204-3366.

INOVA HEALTH SYSTEM — *August*

Staying fit will help you weather the storms and live a long and healthy life. No matter which way the wind blows.

1	T
2	W
3	T
4	F
5	S
6	S
7	M
8	T
9	W
10	T
11	F
12	S
13	S
14	M
15	T
16	W
17	T
18	F
19	S
20	S
21	M
22	T
23	W
24	T
25	F
26	S
27	S
28	M
29	T
30	W

Regular activity such as walking 20 minutes a day can help minimize the health problems associated with aging.

INOVA HEALTH SYSTEM — *November*

From the top down, the pivotal word is balance. Diet with exercise. Work with rest. Prevention with maintenance.

1	F
2	F
3	S
4	S
5	M
6	T
7	W
8	T
9	F
10	S
11	S
12	M
13	T
14	W
15	T
16	F
17	S
18	S
19	M
20	T
21	W
22	T
23	F
24	S
25	S
26	M
27	T
28	W
29	T
30	F
31	S

Inova offers a variety of wellness classes to keep you healthy. Call Inova HealthSource at 703-204-3366.

INOVA HEALTH SYSTEM — *December*

Inova Health System

Health care / For promotional purposes
ヘルス ケア / プロモーション　USA　1994
CD, AD, D: Stephanie Hooton　CD: Jeffrey S. Winter, Jr.
D, I: Hien Nguyen　P: Taran Z　CW: John Frazier / Anne Colt

"COLLECTION OF ALL THAT'S COCA-COLA"

1	2	3	4
JANUARY	FEBRUARY	MARCH	APRIL

SUN	MON	TUE	WED	THU	FRI	SAT
1	2	3	4	5	6	7
8	9	10	11	12	13	14
15	16	17	18	19	20	21
22	23	24	25	26	27	28
29	30	31	•	•	•	•

SUN	MON	TUE	WED	THU	FRI	SAT
			1	2	3	4
5	6	7	8	9	10	11
12	13	14	15	16	17	18
19	20	21	22	23	24	25
26	27	28	•	•	•	•

SUN	MON	TUE	WED	THU	FRI	SAT
			1	2	3	4
5	6	7	8	9	10	11
12	13	14	15	16	17	18
19	20	21	22	23	24	25
26	27	28	29	30	31	•

SUN	MON	TUE	WED	THU	FRI	SAT
						1
2	3	4	5	6	7	8
9	10	11	12	13	14	15
16	17	18	19	20	21	22
23/30	24	25	26	27	28	29

5	6	7	8
MAY	JUNE	JULY	AUGUST

SUN	MON	TUE	WED	THU	FRI	SAT
	1	2	3	4	5	6
7	8	9	10	11	12	13
14	15	16	17	18	19	20
21	22	23	24	25	26	27
28	29	30	31	•	•	•

SUN	MON	TUE	WED	THU	FRI	SAT
				1	2	3
4	5	6	7	8	9	10
11	12	13	14	15	16	17
18	19	20	21	22	23	24
25	26	27	28	29	30	•

SUN	MON	TUE	WED	THU	FRI	SAT
						1
2	3	4	5	6	7	8
9	10	11	12	13	14	15
16	17	18	19	20	21	22
23/30	24/31	25	26	27	28	29

SUN	MON	TUE	WED	THU	FRI	SAT
		1	2	3	4	5
6	7	8	9	10	11	12
13	14	15	16	17	18	19
20	21	22	23	24	25	26
27	28	29	30	31	•	•

9	10	11	12
SEPTEMBER	OCTOBER	NOVEMBER	DECEMBER

SUN	MON	TUE	WED	THU	FRI	SAT
					1	2
3	4	5	6	7	8	9
10	11	12	13	14	15	16
17	18	19	20	21	22	23
24	25	26	27	28	29	30

SUN	MON	TUE	WED	THU	FRI	SAT
1	2	3	4	5	6	7
8	9	10	11	12	13	14
15	16	17	18	19	20	21
22	23	24	25	26	27	28
29	30	31	•	•	•	•

SUN	MON	TUE	WED	THU	FRI	SAT
			1	2	3	4
5	6	7	8	9	10	11
12	13	14	15	16	17	18
19	20	21	22	23	24	25
26	27	28	29	30	•	•

SUN	MON	TUE	WED	THU	FRI	SAT
					1	2
3	4	5	6	7	8	9
10	11	12	13	14	15	16
17	18	19	20	21	22	23
24/31	25	26	27	28	29	30

Coca-Cola® Calendar 1995

Here are some visuals connected with Coca-Cola called "PO-LA-CO-LE" : a collection of Polaroid pictures. "PO-LA-CO-LE" is an original word for a unique
form of art created by Mr. Minato Ishikawa : the Polagraphic artist. Please enjoy the art of Coca-Cola in the color and tone characteristic of Polaroid pictures.

Coca-Cola (Japan) Company, Limited   日本コカ コーラ ㈱

Beverage manufacturer / For promotional purposes   飲料メーカー / プロモーション   Japan 1995
CD: Kazuhiro Takahashi   AD: Yusuke Okabe   D: Tomonori Ouchi   P: Minato Ishikawa
size 983×608 mm

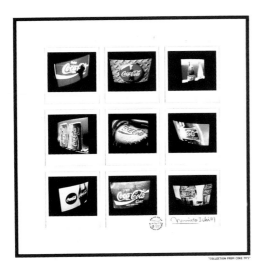

"COLLECTION FROM COKE TV'S"

Coca-Cola® Calendar 1995

Here are some visuals connected with Coca-Cola called "PO-LA-CO-LE": a collection of Polaroid pictures.
"PO-LA-CO-LE" is an original word for a unique form of art created by Mr. Minato Ishikawa : the Polagraphic artist.
Please enjoy the art of Coca-Cola in the color and tone characteristic of Polaroid pictures.

"COLLECTION OF THE COKE RED"

	1	2	3	4	5	6	7				1	2	3	4	
1 JANUARY	8	9	10	11	12	13	14	5	6	7	8	9	10	11	**2** FEBRUARY
	15	16	17	18	19	20	21	12	13	14	15	16	17	18	
	22	23	24	25	26	27	28	19	20	21	22	23	24	25	
	29	30	31					26	27	28					

"COLLECTION FROM SILHOUETTES OF MY FAVORITE THINGS"

			1	2	3	4					1	2	3	4	5	
3 MARCH	5	6	7	8	9	10	11	2	3	4	5	6	7	8	**4** APRIL
	12	13	14	15	16	17	18	9	10	11	12	13	14	15	
	19	20	21	22	23	24	25	16	17	18	19	20	21	22	
	26	27	28	29	30	31		23/30	24	25	26	27	28	29	

"COLLECTION BY THE WINDOW"

							1				1	2	3	4	5	
7 JULY	2	3	4	5	6	7	8	6	7	8	9	10	11	12	**8** AUGUST
	9	10	11	12	13	14	15	13	14	15	16	17	18	19	
	16	17	18	19	20	21	22	20	21	22	23	24	25	26	
	23/30	24/31	25	26	27	28	29	27	28	29	30	31			

Coca-Cola (Japan) Company, Limited 日本コカ コーラ ㈱

Beverage manufacturer / For promotional purposes 飲料メーカー / プロモーション Japan 1995
CD: Kazuhiro Takahashi AD: Yusuke Okabe D: Tomonori Ouchi P: Minato Ishikawa
size 515×515 mm

3

Sun	Mon	Tue	Wed	Thu	Fri	Sat
·	·	1	2	3	4	5
6	7	8	9	10	11	12
13	14	15	16	17	18	19
20	21	22	23	24	25	26
27	28	29	30	31	·	·

4

Sun	Mon	Tue	Wed	Thu	Fri	Sat
·	·	·	·	·	1	2
3	4	5	6	7	8	9
10	11	12	13	14	15	16
17	18	19	20	21	22	23
24	25	26	27	28	29	30

さわやかになる、ひととき。

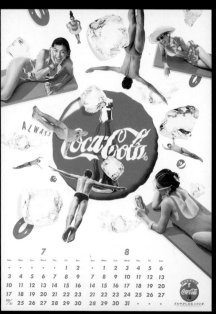

7

Sun	Mon	Tue	Wed	Thu	Fri	Sat
·	·	·	·	·	1	2
3	4	5	6	7	8	9
10	11	12	13	14	15	16
17	18	19	20	21	22	23
24	25	26	27	28	29	30
31						

8

Sun	Mon	Tue	Wed	Thu	Fri	Sat
·	1	2	3	4	5	6
7	8	9	10	11	12	13
14	15	16	17	18	19	20
21	22	23	24	25	26	27
28	29	30	31	·	·	·

9

Sun	Mon	Tue	Wed	Thu	Fri	Sat
·	·	·	·	1	2	3
4	5	6	7	8	9	10
11	12	13	14	15	16	17
18	19	20	21	22	23	24
25	26	27	28	29	30	·

10

Sun	Mon	Tue	Wed	Thu	Fri	Sat
·	·	·	·	·	·	1
2	3	4	5	6	7	8
9	10	11	12	13	14	15
16	17	18	19	20	21	22
23	24	25	26	27	28	29
30	31					

Coca-Cola (Japan) Company, Limited　日本コカ コーラ ㈱

Beverage manufacturer / For promotional purposes　飲料メーカー / プロモーション　Japan　1993
CD: Masayuki Aoki　AD, D: Jun Asano　P: Megumu Wada / Kazunori Tsukada / Takashi Miki

ILLUSTRATION

Raleigh Paper

Paper supplier / For promotional purposes　紙輸入・卸売／プロモーション　Australia 1993
CD, AD, D:Judy Hungerford　P: Paul Henderson-Kelly　I: Tony Pyrzakowski
DF: Judy Hungerford Design Pty Ltd.　size 435×600 mm

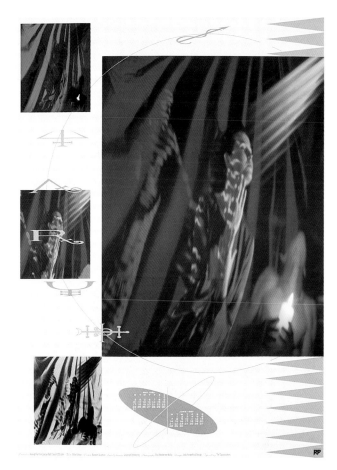

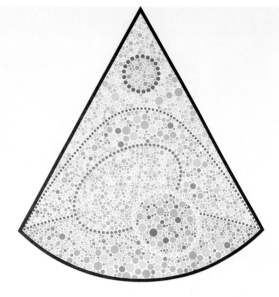

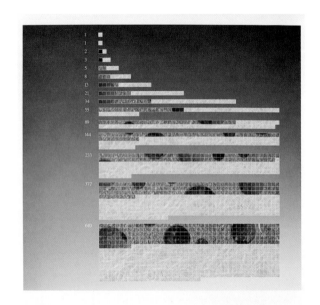

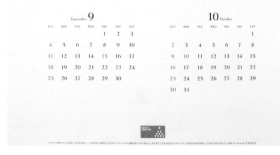

NTT Data Communication Systems Corp.　NTTデータ通信 ㈱

Computer systems development, maintenance, sales, etc. / For promotional purposes
コンピュータ システム開発・保守・販売等 / プロモーション　Japan　1994　CD: Katsumi Nomura
AD: Yuki Hikawa　Artists: Masayoshi Nakajo / Akihiko Tsukamoto / Cornel Windlin /
Katsuhiro Kinoshita / Kijuro Yahagi / Hajime Tachibana　size 483×710 mm

2	S	M	T	W	T	F	S	February
					1	2	3	4
	5	6	7	8	9	10	11	
	12	13	14	15	16	17	18	
	19	20	21	22	23	24	25	
	26	27	28					

March 1 2 3 4 5 6 7 8 9 10 11 12 13 14 15 16 17 18 19 20 21 22 23 24 25 26 27 28 29 30 31

3	S	M	T	W	T	F	S	March
				1	2	3	4	
	5	6	7	8	9	10	11	
	12	13	14	15	16	17	18	
	19	20	21	22	23	24	25	
	26	27	28	29	30	31		

April 1 2 3 4 5 6 7 8 9 10 11 12 13 14 15 16 17 18 19 20 21 22 23 24 25 26 27 28 29 30

CHIBA GAS

8	S	M	T	W	T	F	S	August
			1	2	3	4	5	
	6	7	8	9	10	11	12	
	13	14	15	16	17	18	19	
	20	21	22	23	24	25	26	
	27	28	29	30	31			

September 1 2 3 4 5 6 7 8 9 10 11 12 13 14 15 16 17 18 19 20 21 22 23 24 25 26 27 28 29 30

CHIBA GAS

10	S	M	T	W	T	F	S	October
	1	2	3	4	5	6	7	
	8	9	10	11	12	13	14	
	15	16	17	18	19	20	21	
	22	23	24	25	26	27	28	
	29	30	31					

November 1 2 3 4 5 6 7 8 9 10 11 12 13 14 15 16 17 18 19 20 21 22 23 24 25 26 27 28 29 30

CHIBA GAS

Chiba Gas　千葉ガス

Domestic gas supplier / For promotional purposes　都市ガス供給／プロモーション　Japan　1995
CD, AD, D: Yumi Shirakawa　I: Mei Shirakawa　size 520×360 mm

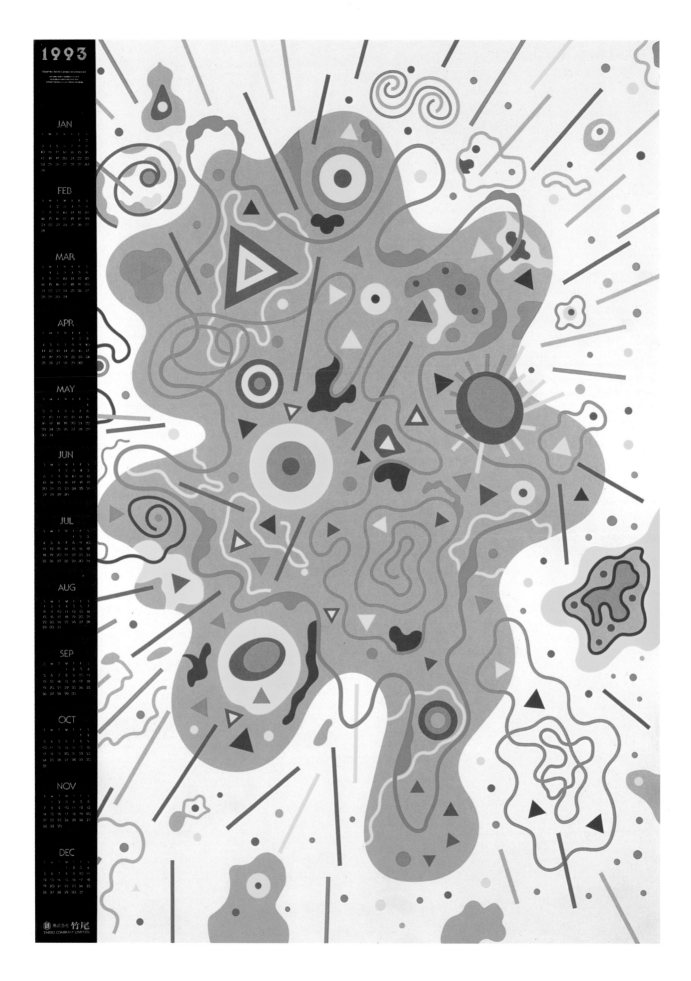

Takeo Co., Ltd. ㈱竹尾

Paper supplier / For promotional purposes　紙卸売／プロモーション　Japan 1993
CD, AD: Yasumichi Uchida　AD, I: You Kitagawa　D: Kokichi Ushiyama
DF: Toppan Printing Co., Ltd. TIC division / Reflex Inc.　size 1025×725 mm

DoCoMo De JAPONISME

1995 NTT DoCoMo Calendar ART by Miha Takagi

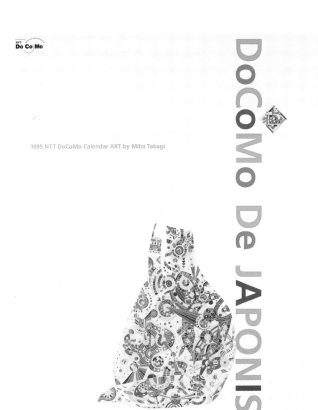

1
JANUARY

S	M	T	W	T	F	S
1	2	3	4	5	6	7
8	9	10	11	12	13	14
15	16	17	18	19	20	21
22	23	24	25	26	27	28
29	30	31				

2
FEBRUARY

S	M	T	W	T	F	S
			1	2	3	4
5	6	7	8	9	10	11
12	13	14	15	16	17	18
19	20	21	22	23	24	25
26	27	28				

5
MAY

S	M	T	W	T	F	S
	1	2	3	4	5	6
7	8	9	10	11	12	13
14	15	16	17	18	19	20
21	22	23	24	25	26	27
28	29	30	31			

6
JUNE

S	M	T	W	T	F	S
				1	2	3
4	5	6	7	8	9	10
11	12	13	14	15	16	17
18	19	20	21	22	23	24
25	26	27	28	29	30	

7
JULY

S	M	T	W	T	F	S
						1
2	3	4	5	6	7	8
9	10	11	12	13	14	15
16	17	18	19	20	21	22
23 30	24 31	25	26	27	28	29

8
AUGUST

S	M	T	W	T	F	S
		1	2	3	4	5
6	7	8	9	10	11	12
13	14	15	16	17	18	19
20	21	22	23	24	25	26
27	28	29	30	31		

NTT Mobile Communications Network Inc.　NTT移動通信網 ㈱

Telecommunications company / For promotional purposes　電信電話 / プロモーション　Japan 1995
CD: NTT Advertising Inc.　CD, DF: Kyodo Printing Co., Ltd. SPC division　AD, I: Miha Takagi
D: You Kitagawa　DF: Reflex Inc.　size 590×420 mm

July 1 2 3 4 5 6 7 8 9 10 11 12 13 14 15 16 17 18 19 20 21 22 23 24 25 26 27 28 29 30 31
August 1 2 3 4 5 6 7 8 9 10 11 12 13 14 15 16 17 18 19 20 21 22 23 24 25 26 27 28 29 30 31

Wacoal Corporation ㈱ ワコール

Lingerie maker / For promotional purposes　インナー ウエア メーカー / プロモーション　Japan 1994
CD, AD: Yutaka Sasaki　CD: Hitoshi Harada　D: Yuji Koiso　I: Masahiro Imai　size 453×557 mm

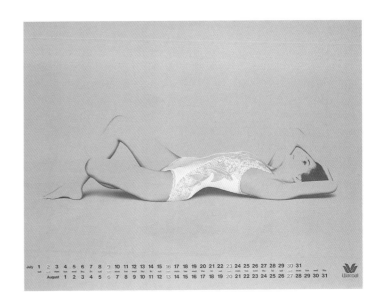

Wacoal Corporation　㈱ ワコール

Lingerie maker / For promotional purposes　インナー ウエア メーカー / プロモーション　Japan　1995
CD, AD: Yutaka Sasaki　CD: Hitoshi Harada　D: Yuji Koiso　P: Kazu Nakamura　I: Masahiro Imai
size 453×557 mm

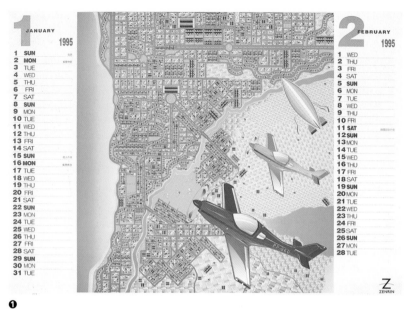

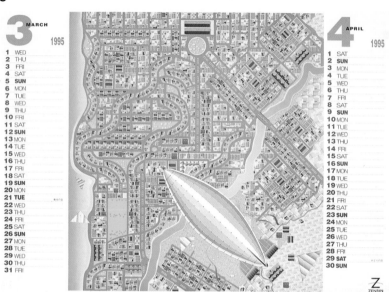

❶

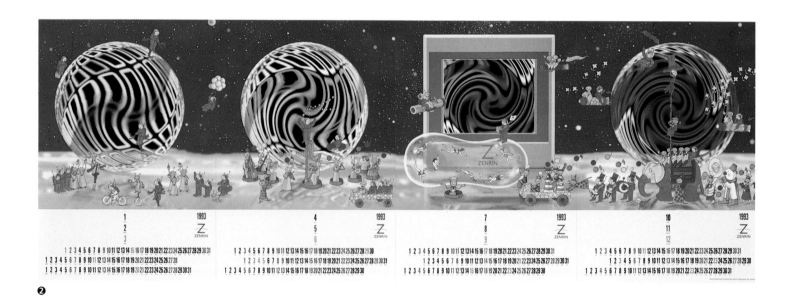

❷

❶
Zenrin ㈱ ゼンリン

City maps and navigation systems supplier / For promotional purposes
住宅地図，ナビゲーション システム製作 / プロモーション　Japan 1995
AD: Atsushi Mori　D: E. Galvani　size 375×515 mm

6	JUNE 1995	
1	THU	
2	FRI	
3	SAT	
4	SUN	
5	MON	
6	TUE	
7	WED	
8	THU	
9	FRI	
10	SAT	
11	SUN	
12	MON	
13	TUE	
14	WED	
15	THU	
16	FRI	
17	SAT	
18	SUN	
19	MON	
20	TUE	
21	WED	
22	THU	
23	FRI	
24	SAT	
25	SUN	
26	MON	
27	TUE	
28	WED	
29	THU	
30	FRI	

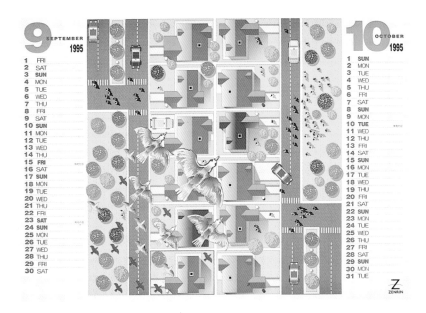

9	SEPTEMBER 1995			10	OCTOBER 1995
1	FRI			1	SUN
2	SAT			2	MON
3	SUN			3	TUE
4	MON			4	WED
5	TUE			5	THU
6	WED			6	FRI
7	THU			7	SAT
8	FRI			8	SUN
9	SAT			9	MON
10	SUN			10	TUE
11	MON			11	WED
12	TUE			12	THU
13	WED			13	FRI
14	THU			14	SAT
15	FRI			15	SUN
16	SAT			16	MON
17	SUN			17	TUE
18	MON			18	WED
19	TUE			19	THU
20	WED			20	FRI
21	THU			21	SAT
22	FRI			22	SUN
23	SAT			23	MON
24	SUN			24	TUE
25	MON			25	WED
26	TUE			26	THU
27	WED			27	FRI
28	THU			28	SAT
29	FRI			29	SUN
30	SAT			30	MON
				31	TUE

8	AUGUST 1995	
1	TUE	
2	WED	
3	THU	
4	FRI	
5	SAT	
6	SUN	
7	MON	
8	TUE	
9	WED	
10	THU	
11	FRI	
12	SAT	
13	SUN	
14	MON	
15	TUE	
16	WED	
17	THU	
18	FRI	
19	SAT	
20	SUN	
21	MON	
22	TUE	
23	WED	
24	THU	
25	FRI	
26	SAT	
27	SUN	
28	MON	
29	TUE	
30	WED	
31	THU	

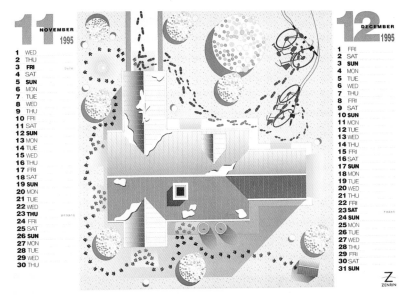

11	NOVEMBER 1995			12	DECEMBER 1995
1	WED			1	FRI
2	THU			2	SAT
3	FRI			3	SUN
4	SAT			4	MON
5	SUN			5	TUE
6	MON			6	WED
7	TUE			7	THU
8	WED			8	FRI
9	THU			9	SAT
10	FRI			10	SUN
11	SAT			11	MON
12	SUN			12	TUE
13	MON			13	WED
14	TUE			14	THU
15	WED			15	FRI
16	THU			16	SAT
17	FRI			17	SUN
18	SAT			18	MON
19	SUN			19	TUE
20	MON			20	WED
21	TUE			21	THU
22	WED			22	FRI
23	THU			23	SAT
24	FRI			24	SUN
25	SAT			25	MON
26	SUN			26	TUE
27	MON			27	WED
28	TUE			28	THU
29	WED			29	FRI
30	THU			30	SAT
				31	SUN

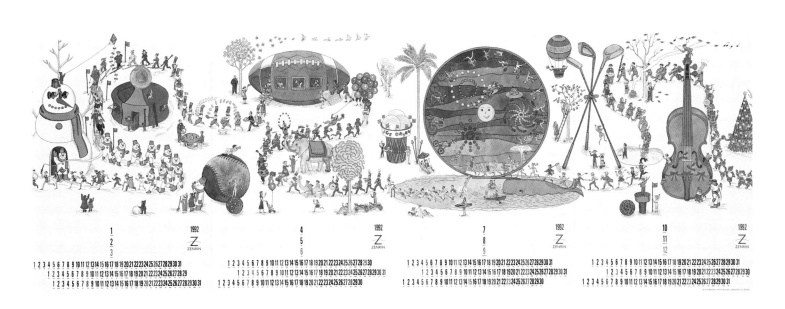

❷
Zenrin ㈱ ゼンリン
City maps and navigation systems supplier / For promotional purposes
住宅地図、ナビゲーション システム製作 / プロモーション　Japan　1992　1993
CD, AD, D: Atsushi Mori　I: Naoyuki Sato　size 1025×360 mm

1995 2 FEBRUARY 5 sun 6 mon 7 tue 8 wed 9 thu 10 fri 11 sat

1995 3 MARCH 12 sun 13 mon 14 tue 15 wed 16 thu 17 fri 18 sat

1995 9 SEPTEMBER 3 sun 4 mon 5 tue 6 wed 7 thu 8 fri 9 sat

1995 6 JUNE 18 sun 19 mon 20 tue 21 wed 22 thu 23 fri 24 sat

Gulliver Co., Ltd. ㈱ガリバー

Printing company / For retail sales　印刷／市販品　Japan 1995
CD: Seiji Koseki　AD: Tatsuomi Majima　D: Akatsuka / Sato / Nakamura / Murata
I: Chizuko Todoroki / Yasushi Nakayama / Hiro Sugiyama / Takato Yamamoto
CW: Megumi Yunoki　DF: A Company Gulliver Book　size 297×210 mm

	JANUARY							
	S	M	T	W	T	F	S	
							1	
2	3	4	5	6	7	8	
9	10	11	12	13	14	15	
16	17	18	19	20	21	22	
23	24	25	26	27	28	29	
30	31						

FEBRUARY

S	M	T	W	T	F	S
		1	2	3	4	5
6	7	8	9	10	11	12
13	14	15	16	17	18	19
20	21	22	23	24	25	26
27	28					

MARCH

S	M	T	W	T	F	S
		1	2	3	4	5
6	7	8	9	10	11	12
13	14	15	16	17	18	19
20	21	22	23	24	25	26
27	28	29	30	31		

APRIL

S	M	T	W	T	F	S
					1	2
3	4	5	6	7	8	9
10	11	12	13	14	15	16
17	18	19	20	21	22	23
24	25	26	27	28	29	30

JULY

S	M	T	W	T	F	S
					1	2
3	4	5	6	7	8	9
10	11	12	13	14	15	16
17	18	19	20	21	22	23
24	25	26	27	28	29	30
31						

AUGUST

S	M	T	W	T	F	S
	1	2	3	4	5	6
7	8	9	10	11	12	13
14	15	16	17	18	19	20
21	22	23	24	25	26	27
28	29	30	31			

It is pathways that transcend
time and worlds.

It is a mission afar
to trade goods and to trade ideas.

and the voice of the people
expressed in a dozen languages.

Port of Seattle

Port authority / For promotional purposes　港湾整備・運営／プロモーション　USA　1994
CD: Margo Spellman　AD, D: Lynn Hernandez　D: Rick Way (Gage Design)　I: Richard Tuschman /
Philippe Weisbecker / Adam Rogers / Jeff Fisher / Pierre La Tan / Linda Frichel　CW: Dick Patzke
DF: Port of Seattle　size 600×228 mm

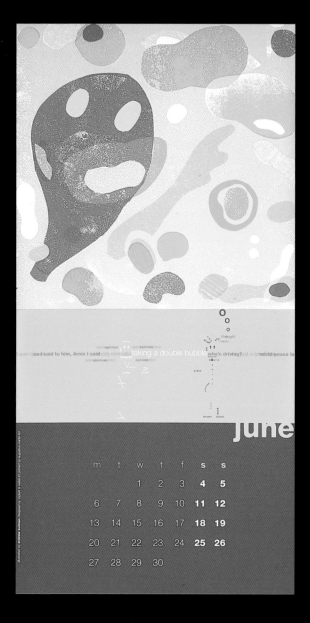

Trickett and Webb / Augustus Martin

Design firm & printing company / For promotional purposes
グラフィック デザイン・印刷 / プロモーション　England　1993-1994
CD, AD, D: Brian Webb / Lynn Trickett　D: Martin Cox　I: Philippe Weisbecker /
Andrew Kulman / Clifford Harper / Peter Blake / Jeff Fisher　CW: Neil Mattingley
DF: Trickett and Webb Limited　size 670×340 mm

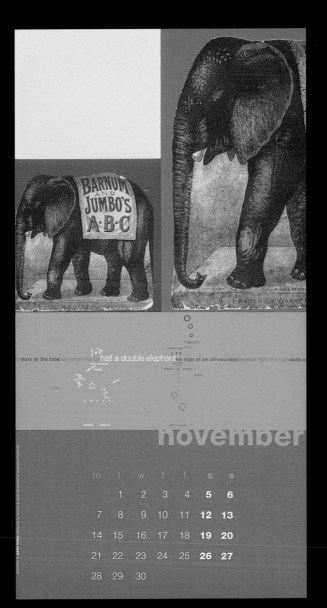

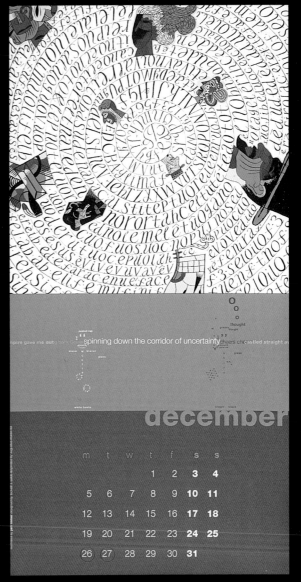

thought

...same again?....our special relationship...

now at the tate...now what i like... half a double elephant...no sign of an all-rounder...tealed right through...sixth...

empire gave me auto...work on... spinning down the corridor of uncertainty...cheers chi...settled straight a...

august

s	s
5 6	7
2 13	14
9 20	21
6 27	28

november

m	t	w	t	f	s	s
	1	2	3	4	**5**	**6**
7	8	9	10	11	**12**	**13**
14	15	16	17	18	**19**	**20**
21	22	23	24	25	**26**	**27**
28	29	30				

december

m	t	w	t	f	s	s
			1	2	**3**	**4**
5	6	7	8	9	**10**	**11**
12	13	14	15	16	**17**	**18**
19	20	21	22	23	**24**	**25**
26	27	28	29	30	**31**	

Timex Corporation

Watch manufacturer / For promotional purposes　腕時計メーカー／プロモーション　USA 1995
CD: Susie Watson　CD, AD: Leslie Evans　AD, D: Mary Brown　P: George Benington /
Peter Macomber Studio　I: Geoffrey P. Smith / Mary Anne Lloyd / Terry Allen / Anne Pickard
DF: Leslie Evans Design Associates　size 210×277mm

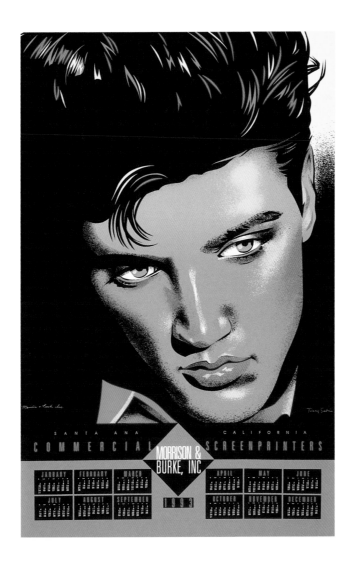

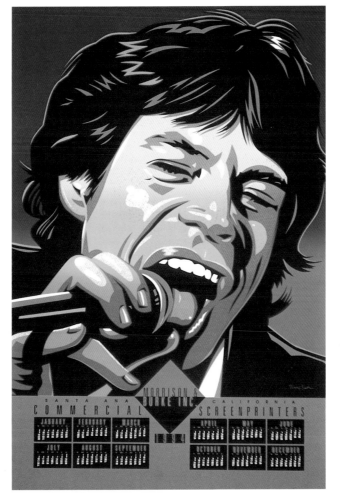

Morrison & Burke Inc.

Printing company / For promotional purposes
印刷／プロモーション
USA 1993 1994
CD: Tom Burke / Tom Morrison
D, I: Tracy Sabin
DF: Sabin Design   size 1092×736 mm

januari

zaterdag 1
zondag 2
maandag 3
dinsdag 4
woensdag 5
6
donderdag 7
vrijdag 8
zaterdag 9
zondag 10
maandag 11
dinsdag 12
woensdag 13
donderdag 14
vrijdag 15
16
zaterdag 17
zondag 18
maandag 19
dinsdag 20
woensdag 21
donderdag 22
vrijdag 23
zaterdag 24
zondag 25
maandag 26
dinsdag 27
woensdag 28
donderdag 29
vrijdag 30
zaterdag 31
zondag
maandag

doodshoofdaapje Zoals wel vaker, speelt ook hier de televisie een rol bij de handel in een dier: Lang leve Pippi Langkous. Met kisten vol werden ze ontvoerd, slechts een enkeling overleefde de barre reis en zit nu in een parkietenkooitje. Of bij Stichting A A P.

november

meerkat

maart

capucijnaap

Animal Support

Charity organization / For promotional purposes　チャリティー団体 / プロモーション
Netherlands　1994　CD, D: André Toet　D: Mike Otten　I: Frank Dam / Bart van Leeuwen /
Tom saecker　CW: Jan van der Lee　DF: Samenwerkende Ontwerpers bv　size 400 × 500 mm

May

August

November

The City Magazine

Magazine publisher / For promotional purposes　雑誌出版／プロモーション　USA　1993
AD, D: Scott Kambic　I: Eric White　size 275×215 mm

Vue sur la Ville

Graphic design firm / For promotional purposes   グラフィック デザイン / プロモーション
France 1994   CD, AD, D: Alain Lachartre   I: Lorenzo Mattotti / Marcellino Truong / Richard Beards /
Martin Jarrie   size 360×280 mm

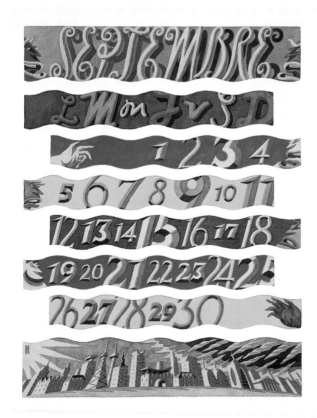

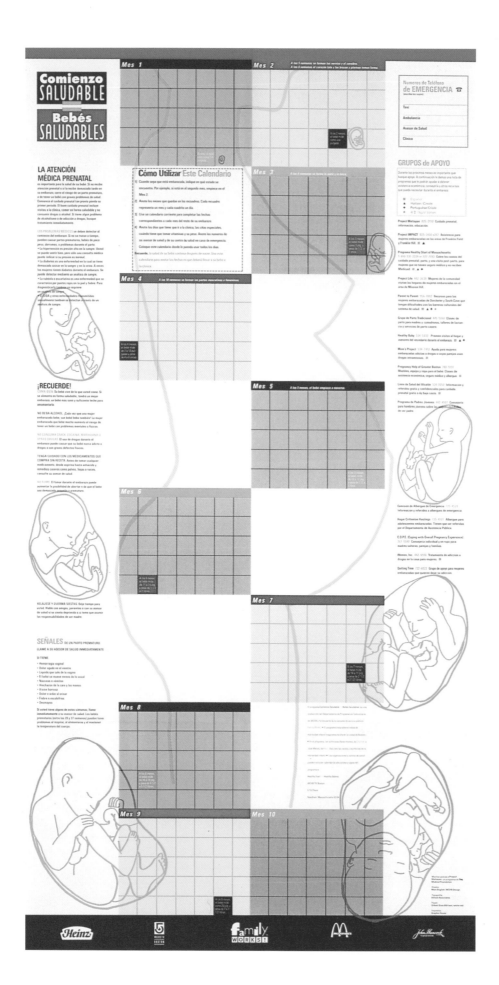

WCVB TV Boston

TV network / For promotional purposes   TV局／プロモーション   USA 1992
AD, D, I: Marc English   CW: Karen Holmes   DF: Marc English: Design   size 1215×610 mm

Schowalter 2 Design

Graphic design firm / For promotional purposes　グラフィック デザイン／プロモーション　USA　1992
CD, AD: Toni Schowalter　D: Ilene Price　CW: Colin Goedecke　DF: Schowalter 2 Design
size 137×825 mm

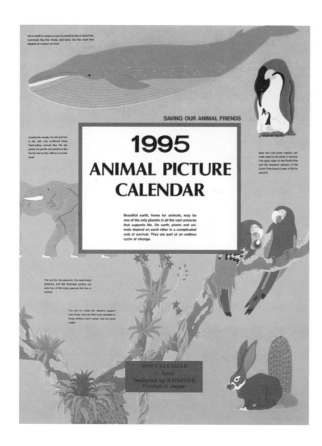

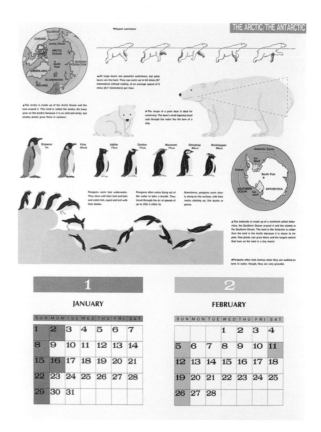

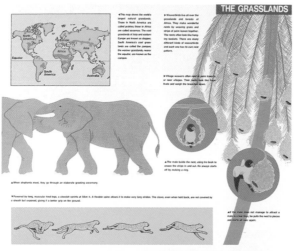

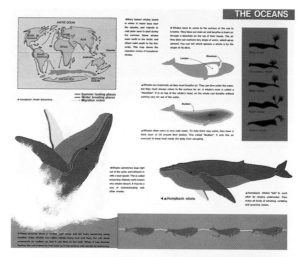

Æsop Co., Ltd.　㈱ イソップ

Stationery supplier / For retail sales　雑貨、ステーショナリー製造・販売 / 市販品　Japan　1995
CD: Planning Dept., Æsop　D: Kanaya Sugiyama　size 520×385 mm

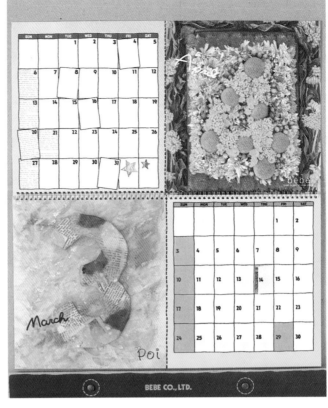

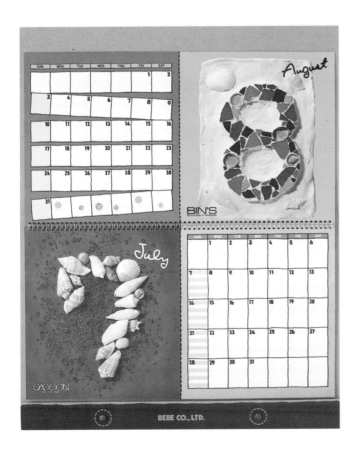

BeBe Co., Ltd. ㈱ べべ

Apparel maker / For promotional purposes　アパレル メーカー / プロモーション　Japan　1994
CD, AD, P: Yarakasukan Inc.　D: BeBe Co., Ltd.　size 540×440 mm

1994			1			
SUN	MON	TUE	WED	THU	FRI	SAT
26	27	28	29	30	31	1
2	3	4	5	6	7	8
9	10	11	12	13	14	15
16	17	18	19	20	21	22
23 30	24 31	25	26	27	28	29

illustration by **TETSURO OKABE**

1994			2			
SUN	MON	TUE	WED	THU	FRI	SAT
30	31	1	2	3	4	5
6	7	8	9	10	11	12
13	14	15	16	17	18	19
20	21	22	23	24	25	26
27	28	1	2	3	4	5

illustration by **TETSURO OKABE**

❶

1994			7			
SUN	MON	TUE	WED	THU	FRI	SAT
26	27	28	29	30	1	2
3	4	5	6	7	8	9
10	11	12	13	14	15	16
17	18	19	20	21	22	23
24 31	25	26	27	28	29	30

illustration by **TETSURO OKABE**

1994			11			
SUN	MON	TUE	WED	THU	FRI	SAT
30	31	1	2	3	4	5
6	7	8	9	10	11	12
13	14	15	16	17	18	19
20	21	22	23	24	25	26
27	28	29	30	1	2	3

illustration by **TETSURO OKABE**

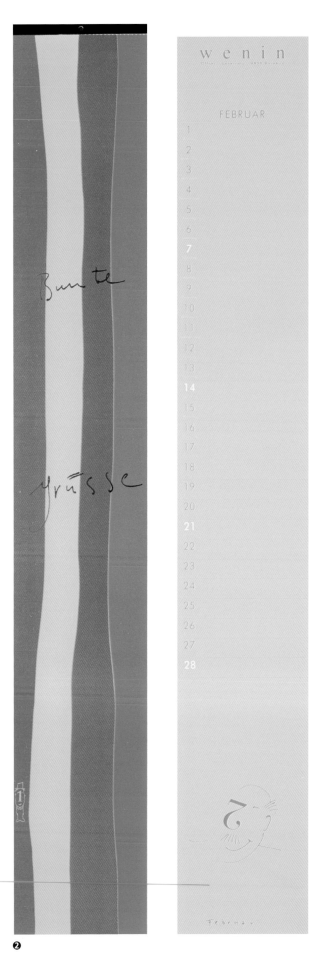

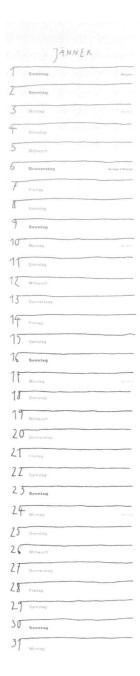

JÄNNER

❷

❶

Pardo Inc. ㈱パルド

Graphic design firm / For promotional purposes　グラフィックデザイン／プロモーション　Japan　1994
AD, D, I: Tetsuro Okabe　size 220×105 mm

❷

Wenin Ohg

Printing company / For promotional purposes　印刷／プロモーション　Austria　1993 1994
AD, D, I, CW: Sigi Ramoser　size 195×700 mm

❶

❷

❶ Osaka city government 大阪市

City government / For promotional purposes 大阪市／プロモーション Japan 1994
CD: Akaya Nakai AD: Miyo Maeda D: Hikaru Adachi I: Mariko Abe CW: Tadayuki Inoue
DF: OAD size 250×360 mm

❷ Misawa Homes Co., Ltd. ミサワホーム ㈱

Construction company / For promotional purposes 建設／プロモーション Japan 1995
AD, D: Akio Sasagawa Artwork: Atsuko Harigai DF: SD Room Inc. size 505×450 mm

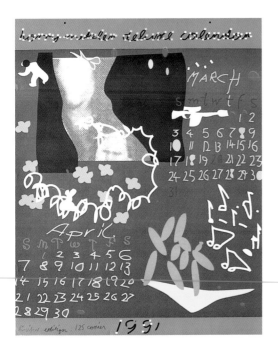

Ian Woodner Family Collection

Art collection / For promotional purposes　アート コレクター / プロモーション　Austria　1991
CD, AD, D: Harry Metzler　CW: Walter Koschatzky　Editor: Veronika Birke
DF: Harry Metzler Artdesign　size 600×480 mm

Kunio Sato

Original

1994

*

Calendar

						1
2	3	4	5	6	7	8
9	10	11	12	13	14	15
16	17	18	19	20	21	22
23	24	25	26	27	28	29
30	31					

January **1**

				1	2	3	4
5	6	7	8	9	10	11
12	13	14	15	16	17	18
19	20	21	22	23	24	25
26	27	28	29	30		

6 June

	1	2	3	4	5	6
7	8	9	10	11	12	13
14	15	16	17	18	19	20
21	22	23	24	25	26	27
28	29	30	31			

8 August

Spoon Co., Ltd. ㈱スプーン

Illustrators / For retail sales　イラストレーション / 市販品　Japan 1994
D: Jun Sato　I: Kunio Sato　size 375×250 mm

			1								2			
SUN	MON	TUE	WED	THU	FRI	SAT		SUN	MON	TUE	WED	THU	FRI	SAT
1	2	3	4	5	6	7				1	2	3	4
8	9	10	11	12	13	14		5	6	7	8	9	10	11
15	16	17	18	19	20	21		12	13	14	15	16	17	18
22	23	24	25	26	27	28		19	20	21	22	23	24	25
29	30	31						26	27	28				

SAIS⊕N
セゾン生命

❶

			5								6			
SUN	MON	TUE	WED	THU	FRI	SAT		SUN	MON	TUE	WED	THU	FRI	SAT
	1	2	3	4	5	6					1	2	3
7	8	9	10	11	12	13		4	5	6	7	8	9	10
14	15	16	17	18	19	20		11	12	13	14	15	16	17
21	22	23	24	25	26	27		18	19	20	21	22	23	24
28	29	30	31					25	26	27	28	29	30	

SAIS⊕N
セゾン生命

3 March
1995
April 4

日産自動車株式会社

❷

11 November
1995
December 12

日産自動車株式会社

❶ Saison Life Insurance Co., Ltd.　セゾン生命保険 ㈱

Insurance company / For promotional purposes　生命保険 / プロモーション　Japan 1995
CD: Shunichi Iwasaki　CD, AD: Kaoru Kasai　D: Youko Inoue / Mayumi Kawahara
I: Masayoshi Nakajo　size 540×420 mm

❷ Nissan Motor Co., Ltd.　日産自動車 ㈱

Auto maker / For promotional purposes　自動車メーカー / プロモーション　Japan 1995
Planning: Nissan Motor Co., Ltd.　DF: Nissan Graphic Arts Co., Ltd.　size 257×298 mm

❶

❷

❶

WCVB TV Boston

TV network / For promotional purposes　TV局／プロモーション　USA 1992
AD, D: Marc English　CW: Judy Foy　DF: Marc English: Design　size 455×280 mm

❷

Honma Golf Co., Ltd.　㈱ 本間ゴルフ

Golfing goods manufacturer / For promotional purposes　ゴルフ用品メーカー／プロモーション　Japan 1995
CD: Vallira Japan Inc.　D: Haruyasu Andoh　I: Minoru Hozumi　size 450×700 mm

Jan.
1 2 3 4 5 6 7
8 9 10 11 12 13 14
15 16 17 18 19 20 21
22 23 24 25 26 27 28
29 30 31

Feb.
1 2 3 4
5 6 7 8 9 10 11
12 13 14 15 16 17 18
19 20 21 22 23 24 25
26 27 28

Mar.
1 2 3 4
5 6 7 8 9 10 11
12 13 14 15 16 17 18
19 20 21 22 23 24 25
26 27 28 29 30 31

Apr.
1
2 3 4 5 6 7 8
9 10 11 12 13 14 15
16 17 18 19 20 21 22
23 24 25 26 27 28 29
30

Jul.
1
2 3 4 5 6 7 8
9 10 11 12 13 14 15
16 17 18 19 20 21 22
23 24 25 26 27 28 29
30 31

Aug.
1 2 3 4 5
6 7 8 9 10 11 12
13 14 15 16 17 18 19
20 21 22 23 24 25 26
27 28 29 30 31

Nov.
1 2 3 4
5 6 7 8 9 10 11
12 13 14 15 16 17 18
19 20 21 22 23 24 25
26 27 28 29 30

Dec.
1 2
3 4 5 6 7 8 9
10 11 12 13 14 15 16
17 18 19 20 21 22 23
24 25 26 27 28 29 30
31

Planning & Direction Inc. ㈱ プランニング & ディレクション

Graphic design & advertising / For promotional purposes
グラフィック デザイン・広告制作 / プロモーション　Japan　1995
CD, AD: Tetsuo Yayoshi　D: Fumiko Nagase　I: Hisashi Saitoh　DF: Planning & Direction Inc.
size 525×360 mm

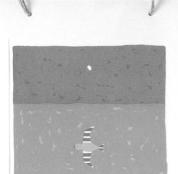

Calendar
1995

Caoru Goto

Art Print Japan Co., Ltd. ㈱アートプリントジャパン

Stationery supplier / For retail sales　ポスター、カード製造・販売 / 市販品　Japan 1995
BR: graphic station　D: Mutsuko Morita　I: Caoru Goto　size 395×255 mm

❶

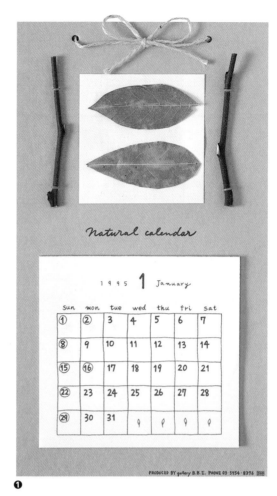

❶

❷

❸

❶
Art Print Japan Co., Ltd. ㈱アートプリントジャパン

Stationery supplier / For retail sales　ポスター、カード製造・販売／市販品
Japan 1995　BR: graphic station　D: Mutsuko Morita　size 285×165 mm

❷
Art Print Japan Co., Ltd. ㈱アートプリントジャパン

Stationery supplier / For retail sales　ポスター、カード製造・販売／市販品
Japan 1995　BR: graphic station　D: Yuko Nagasue　size 275×196 mm

❸
Art Print Japan Co., Ltd. ㈱アートプリントジャパン

Stationery supplier / For retail sales　ポスター、カード製造・販売／市販品
Japan 1995　BR: graphic station　D: Reiko Sumi　size 262×160 mm

1

						1
2	3	4	5	6	7	8
9	10	11	12	13	14	15
16	17	18	19	20	21	22
23	24	25	26	27	28	29
30	31					

2

				1	2	3	4	5
6	7	8	9	10	11	12
13	14	15	16	17	18	19
20	21	22	23	24	25	26
27	28					

3

		1	2	3	4	5
6	7	8	9	10	11	12
13	14	15	16	17	18	19
20	21	22	23	24	25	26
27	28	29	30	31		

4

					1	2
3	4	5	6	7	8	9
10	11	12	13	14	15	16
17	18	19	20	21	22	23
24	25	26	27	28	29	30

5

1	2	3	4	5	6	7
8	9	10	11	12	13	14
15	16	17	18	19	20	21
22	23	24	25	26	27	28
29	30	31				

6

			1	2	3	4
5	6	7	8	9	10	11
12	13	14	15	16	17	18
19	20	21	22	23	24	25
26	27	28	29	30		

7

					1	2
3	4	5	6	7	8	9
10	11	12	13	14	15	16
17	18	19	20	21	22	23
24	25	26	27	28	29	30
31						

8

	1	2	3	4	5	6
7	8	9	10	11	12	13
14	15	16	17	18	19	20
21	22	23	24	25	26	27
28	29	30	31			

9

				1	2	3
4	5	6	7	8	9	10
11	12	13	14	15	16	17
18	19	20	21	22	23	24
25	26	27	28	29	30	

10

						1
2	3	4	5	6	7	8
9	10	11	12	13	14	15
16	17	18	19	20	21	22
23	24	25	26	27	28	29
30	31					

11

	1	2	3	4	5
6	7	8	9	10	11	12
13	14	15	16	17	18	19
20	21	22	23	24	25	26
27	28	29	30			

12

				1	2	3
4	5	6	7	8	9	10
11	12	13	14	15	16	17
18	19	20	21	22	23	24
25	26	27	28	29	30	31

Harumin Asao 浅生ハルミン

Graphic designer / For private use　グラフィック デザイン / プライベート　Japan 1994
AD, D: Chiaki Kawai　I: Harumin Asao　size 155×70 mm

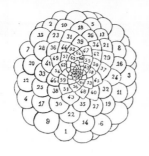

JANUARY

s	m	t	w	t	f	s
			1	2	3	4
5	6	7	8	9	10	11
12	13	14	15	16	17	18
19	20	21	22	23	24	25
26	27	28	29	30	31	

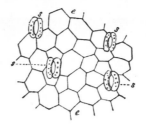

JUNE

s	m	t	w	t	f	s
	1	2	3	4	5	6
7	8	9	10	11	12	13
14	15	16	17	18	19	20
21	22	23	24	25	26	27
28	29	30				

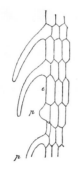

AUGUST

s	m	t	w	t	f	s
						1
2	3	4	5	6	7	8
9	10	11	12	13	14	15
16	17	18	19	20	21	22
23	24	25	26	27	28	29
30	31					

NOVEMBER

s	m	t	w	t	f	s
1	2	3	4	5	6	7
8	9	10	11	12	13	14
15	16	17	18	19	20	21
22	23	24	25	26	27	28
29	30					

Eriko Kashiwagi　柏木 江里子

Graphic designer / For promotional purposes　グラフィック デザイン／プロモーション　Japan 1992
AD, D: Eriko Kashiwagi　size 420×295 mm

décembre

dim	lun	mar	mer	jeu	ven	sam
✳	✳	✳	✳	✳	1	2
3	4	5	6	7	8	9
10	11	12	13	14	15	16
17	18	19	20	21	22	23
24/31	25	26	27	28	29	30

février

dim	lun	mar	mer	jeu	ven	sam
✳	✳	✳	1	2	3	4
5	6	7	8	9	10	11
12	13	14	15	16	17	18
19	20	21	22	23	24	25
26	27	28	✳	✳	✳	✳

mars

dim	lun	mar	mer	jeu	ven	sam
✳	✳	✳	1	2	3	4
5	6	7	8	9	10	11
12	13	14	15	16	17	18
19	20	21	22	23	24	25
26	27	28	29	30	31	✳

Gulliver Co., Ltd.　㈱ガリバー

Printing company / For retail sales　印刷／市販品　Japan 1995
CD, DF: A Company Gulliver Book　AD, I: Rica Takada　size 257×182 mm

January. **1** 1995

SUN	MON	TUE	WED	THU	FRI	SAT
① NEW YEAR'S DAY.	②	3	4	5	6	7
8	9	10	11	12	13	14
⑮ ADULT'S DAY.	⑯	17	18	19	20	21
22	23	24	25	26	27	28
29	30	31	1	2	3	4
5	6	7				

Bonjour, voici nos trois enfants.

february. **2** 1995

SUN	MON	TUE	WED	THU	FRI	SAT
29	30	31	1	2	3	4
5	6	7	8	9	10	⑪ NATIONAL FOUNDATION DAY
12	13	14 ST VALENTINE'S DAY	15	16	17	18
19	20	21	22	23	24	25
26	27	28	1	2	3	4
5	6	7				

Nous nous promenons dans le parc.

March. **3** 1995

SUN	MON	TUE	WED	THU	FRI	SAT
26	27	28	1	2	3	4
5	6	7	8	9	10	11
12	13	14 WHITE DAY	15	16	17	18
19	20	㉑ VERNAL EQUINOX DAY.	22	23	24	25
26	27	28	29	30	31	1
2	3	4				

Art Print Japan Co., Ltd. ㈱アートプリントジャパン

Stationery supplier / For retail sales　ポスター、カード製造・販売／市販品　Japan 1995
BR: graphic station　D: Mutsuko Morita　I: Rari Yoshio　size 520×385 mm

❶
Æsop Co., Ltd.　㈱ イソップ

Stationery supplier / For retail sales　雑貨、ステーショナリー製造・販売 / 市販品　Japan　1995
CD: Planning Dept., Æsop　size 265×265 mm

❷
Æsop Co., Ltd.　㈱ イソップ

Stationery supplier / For retail sales　雑貨、ステーショナリー製造・販売 / 市販品　Japan　1995
CD: Planning Dept., Æsop　D: Tomoko Sakaime　size 265×265 mm

JANUARY

A tortoise and a hare started to dispute which of them was the swifter, and before separating they made an appointment for a certain time and place to settle the matter. The hare had such confidence in it's natural fleetness that it did not trouble about the race but lay down by the wayside and went to sleep. The tortoise acutely conscious of its slow movements, padded along without ever stopping until it passed the hare and won the race.

SUN.	MON.	TUE.	WED.	THU.	FRI.	SAT.
NEW YEAR'S DAY 1995.1.1	2	3	4	5	6	7
8	9	10	11	12	13	14
COMING-OF-AGE DAY 15	16	17	18	19	20	21
22	23	24	25	26	27	28
29	30	31				

¶ A naturally gifted man, through lack of application, is often beaten by a plodder.

APRIL

A dog was crossing over a river with a piece of meat in her mouth. Seeing her own reflection in the water she thought it was another dog with a bigger piece of meat. So she dropped her own piece and made a spring to snatch the piece that the other dog had. The result was that she had neither. She could not get the other piece because it did not exist, and her own was swept down by the current.

SUN.	MON.	TUE.	WED.	THU.	FRI.	SAT.
		¶ This tale shows what happens to people who always want more than they have.				APRIL FOOLS' DAY 1995.4.1
2	3	4	5	6	7	8
9	10	11	12	13	14	15
16	17	18	19	20	21	22
23	24	25	26	27	28	29
30						GREENERY DAY

JULY

A man believed that he could read the future in the stars. One evening he was walking the open road. His eyes were fixed on the stars. He thought he saw there that the end of the world was at hand, when all at once, down he went into a hole. The villagers heard him and came. As they pulled him out of the hole, one of them said; 'What use is it to read the stars, when you can't see what right here on the earth?'

SUN.	MON.	TUE.	WED.	THU.	FRI.	SAT.
						1995.7.1
2	3	4	5	6	7 STAR'S FESTIVAL	8
9	10	11	12	13	14	15
16	17	18	19	20	21	22
23	24					
30	31	25	26	27	28	29

OCTOBER

A lion was captured by hunters, he was tied by rope to a tree. A mouse which had been saved his life by the lion heard his groans and running to the spot freed him by gnawing through the rope. 'You laughed at me the other day,' it said, 'because you did not expect me to repay your kindness. Now you see that even mice are graceful.'

SUN.	MON.	TUE.	WED.	THU.	FRI.	SAT.
1995.10.1	2	3	4	5	6	7
8	9	10 SPORTS DAY	11	12	13	14
15	16	17	18	19	20	21
22	23	24 HALLOWEEN	25	26	27	28
29	30	31				

¶ A change of fortune can make the strongest man need a weaker man's help.

Æsop Co., Ltd.　㈱イソップ

Stationery supplier / For retail sales　雑貨、ステーショナリー製造・販売 / 市販品　Japan　1995
CD: Planning Dept., Æsop　D: Yumiko Fukunaga　size 230×190 mm

Let's go for a morning walk!

We had a baseball game with his team yesterday.

March
S M T W T F S
            1 2 3 4
5 6 7 8 9 10 11
12 13 14 15 16 17 18
19 20 21 22 ·23 24 25
26 27 28 29 30 31

May
S M T W T F S
         1 2 3 4 5 6
7 8 9 10 11 12 13
14 15 16 17 18 19 20
21 22 23 24 25 26 27
28 29 30 31

Æsop Co., Ltd.　㈱ イソップ

Stationery supplier / For retail sales　雑貨、ステーショナリー製造・販売 / 市販品　Japan 1995
CD: Planning Dept., Æsop　D: Akiko Ehara / Mico Ogura　size 295×165 mm

1 January

1	SUN	New Year's Day
2	MON	
3	TUE	
4	WED	
5	THU	
6	FRI	
7	SAT	
8	SUN	
9	MON	
10	TUE	
11	WED	
12	THU	
13	FRI	
14	SAT	
15	SUN	Coming-of-Age Day
16	MON	
17	TUE	
18	WED	
19	THU	
20	FRI	
21	SAT	
22	SUN	
23	MON	
24	TUE	
25	WED	
26	THU	
27	FRI	
28	SAT	
29	SUN	
30	MON	
31	TUE	

4 April

1	SAT	April Fools' Day
2	SUN	
3	MON	
4	TUE	
5	WED	
6	THU	
7	FRI	
8	SAT	
9	SUN	
10	MON	
11	TUE	
12	WED	
13	THU	
14	FRI	
15	SAT	
16	SUN	
17	MON	
18	TUE	
19	WED	
20	THU	
21	FRI	
22	SAT	
23	SUN	
24	MON	
25	TUE	
26	WED	
27	THU	
28	FRI	
29	SAT	Greenery Day
30	SUN	

6 June

1	THU	
2	FRI	
3	SAT	
4	SUN	
5	MON	
6	TUE	
7	WED	
8	THU	
9	FRI	
10	SAT	
11	SUN	
12	MON	
13	TUE	
14	WED	
15	THU	
16	FRI	
17	SAT	
18	SUN	Father's Day
19	MON	
20	TUE	
21	WED	
22	THU	
23	FRI	
24	SAT	
25	SUN	
26	MON	
27	TUE	
28	WED	
29	THU	
30	FRI	

Æsop Co., Ltd. ㈱ イソップ

Stationery supplier / For retail sales　雑貨、ステーショナリー製造・販売 / 市販品　Japan 1995
CD: Planning Dept., Æsop　size 440×100 mm

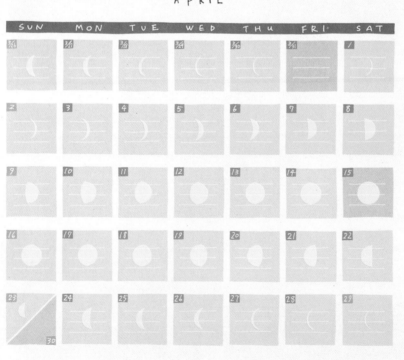

Art Print Japan Co., Ltd. ㈱アートプリントジャパン

Stationery supplier / For retail sales　ポスター、カード製造・販売 / 市販品　Japan 1995
BR: graphic station　　D, I: Chikae Kobayashi　size 365×350 mm

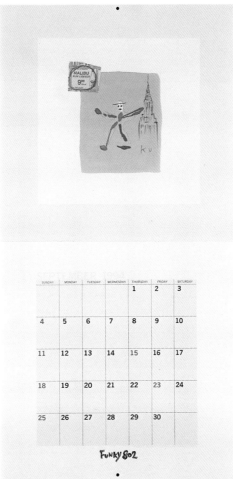

FM802 ㈱ FM802

FM radio station / For promotional purposes FM放送局 / プロモーション Japan 1994
AD: Keisuke Nagatomo D: Shigeki Kato I: Seitaro Kuroda DF: K2 size 490×250 mm

TYPOGRAPHY

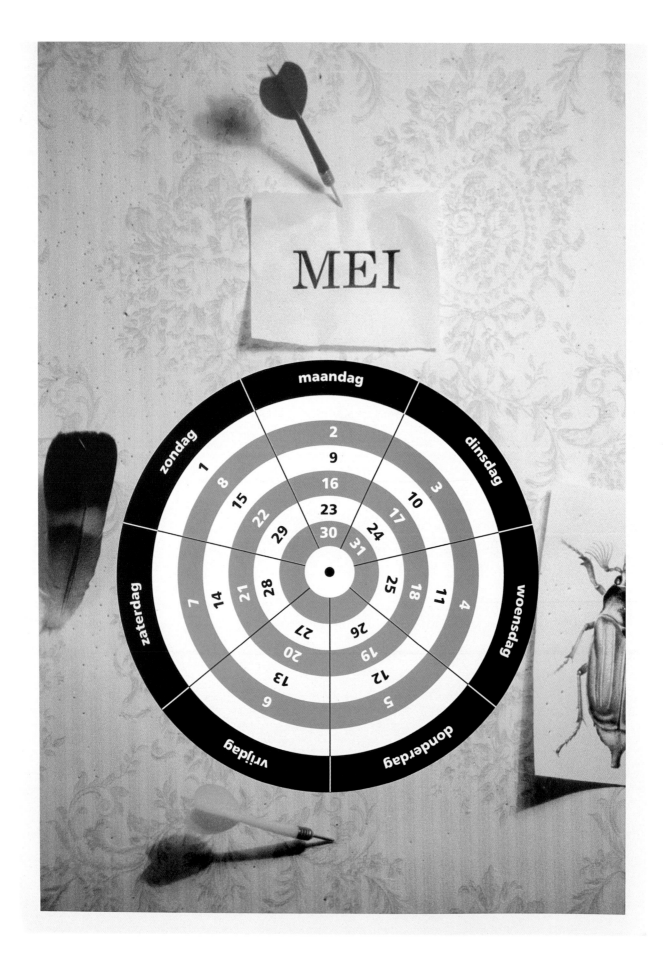

Herman Grasman / Jan Sevenster / Arjen Boschma / Maaik Hamelynck /
Karin Koelma / Geja Duiker / Marjan Peeters / Gertjan van Leeuwen /
Noud van Spaadonk / Marleen Zoon / Edvard Mlinar / Douwe Huitema /
Marga Scholma

Graphic designers / For promotional purposes   グラフィック デザイン / プロモーション
Netherlands 1994   I: Meinte Strikwerda (cover)   size 420×594 mm

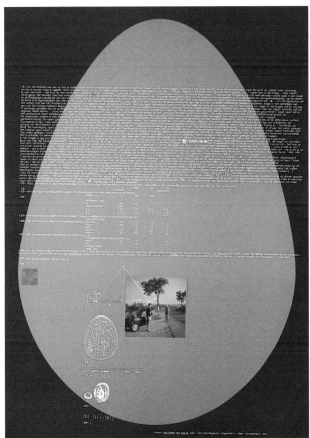

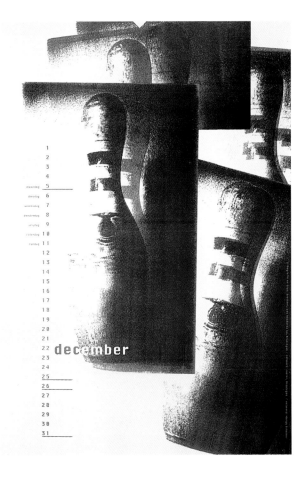

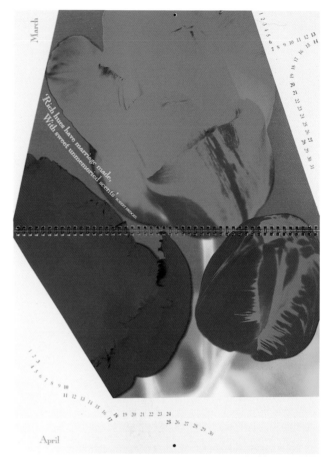

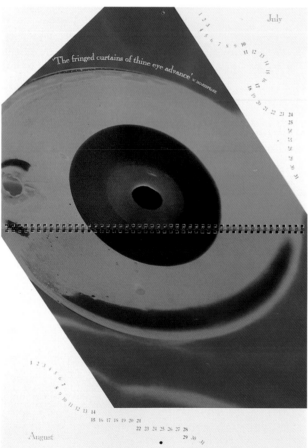

Through the Lens Pty. Ltd.

Photographic services / For promotional purposes　フォト サービス / プロモーション　Australia 1993
AD, P: Anita Marks　CW: Quotes from Famous Poets　DF: Amanda Roach Design Pty. Ltd.
size 600×420 mm

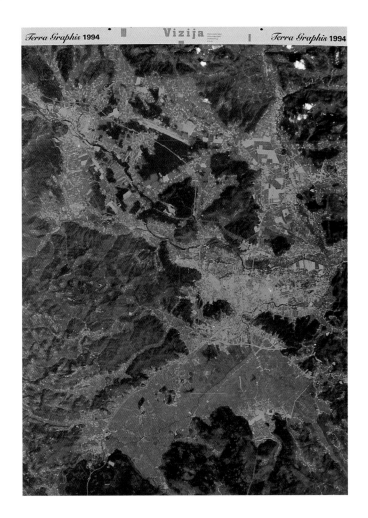

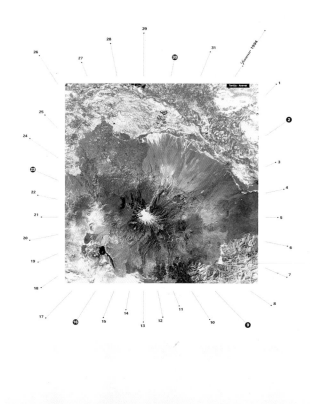

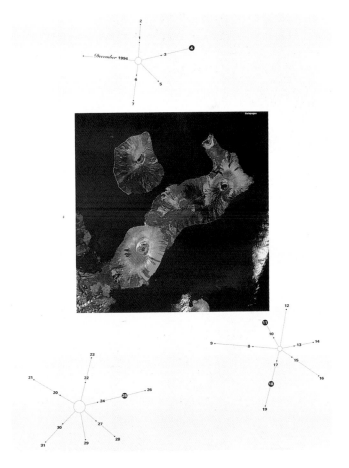

Vizija

Computer engineering / For promotional purposes　コンピュータ サービス / プロモーション　Slovenia　1994
CD: Andrej Jerovšek　D: Radovan Jenko　P: Spot Images by Explorer　DF: Kodia Photo & Graphis
size 550×470 mm

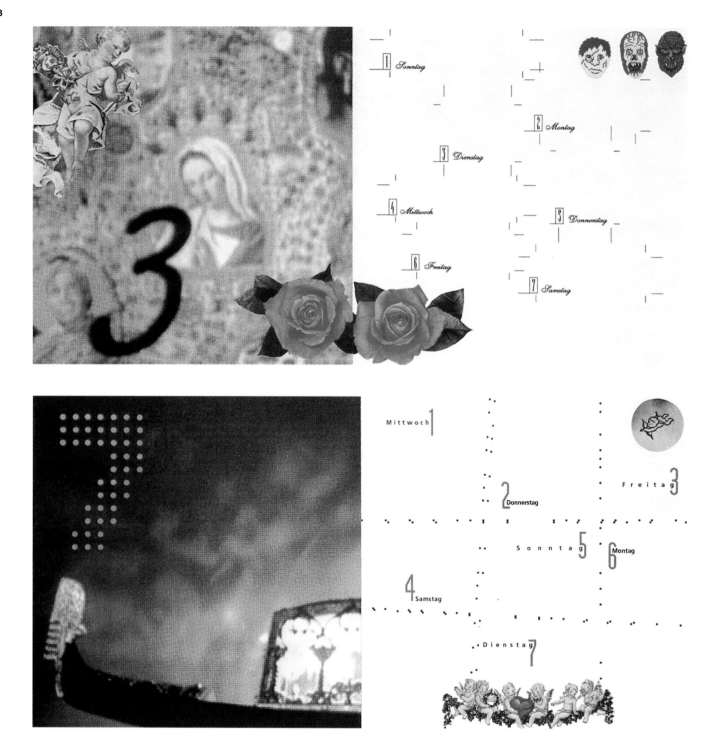

Eva Walter Design

Graphic design firm / For private use　グラフィック デザイン / プライベート　Germany 1991
CD, AD, D, P, I, CW: Eva Walter Design　size 170×340 mm

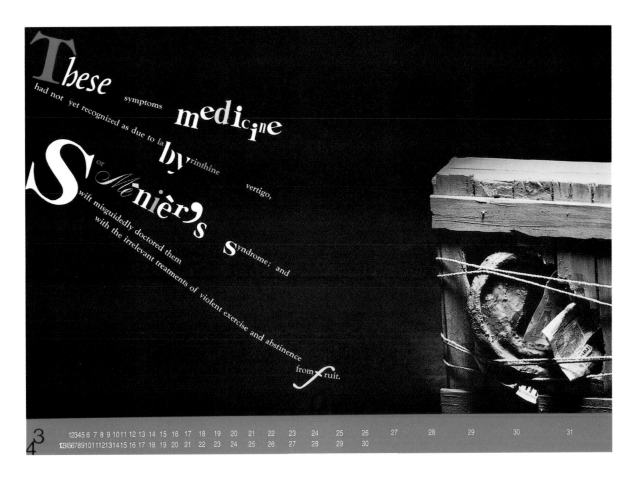

Designer's Arc デザイナーズ アルク

Graphic design firm / For promotional purposes　グラフィック デザイン / プロモーション
Japan　1993　CD: Yuki Matano　D, I: Shoichi Matano　P: Masaru Kusaki　size 295×420 mm

Juli

Augustus 1993

WEEK 30

26 Maandag

27 Dinsdag

28 Woensdag

29 Donderdag

30 Vrijdag

31 Zaterdag

1 Zondag

WEEK 31

2 Maandag

3 Dinsdag

4 Woensdag

5 Donderdag

6 Vrijdag

7 Zaterdag

8 Zondag

De samenstelli

Que sera, sera

When I was just a little girl,
I asked my mother, "What will I be?
Will I be pretty?
Will I be rich?"
Here's what she said to me:

"Que sera, sera,
Whatever will be, will be
The future is not ours to see.
Que sera, sera,
What will be, will be."

When I was just a child at school,
I asked my theacher, "What should I try?
Should I paint pictures?
Should I sing songs?"
This was her wise reply:

"Que sera, sera,
Whatever will be, will be
The future is not ours to see.
Que sera, sera,
What will be, will be."

When I grew up and fell in love,
I asked my lover, "What lies ahead?
Will we have rainbows?
Day after day?"
Here's what my lover said :

"Que sera, sera,
Whatever will be, will be
The future is not ours to see.
Que sera, sera,
What will be, will be."

The Plantijn Group

Printing company / For promotional purposes　印刷 / プロモーション　Netherlands 1993
CD, D, P: Arno Bauman　D: Emmy van Harskamp / Ivo van Leeuwen / Brigitte van Loon / Jan Pinto /
Inge van der Ploeg / Sylvia Suyker / Claudia Vermeulen　I: Gebroeders Das / René van Halderen
CW: Ronald Lagendijk　DF: Studio Bauman bNO　size 580×450 mm

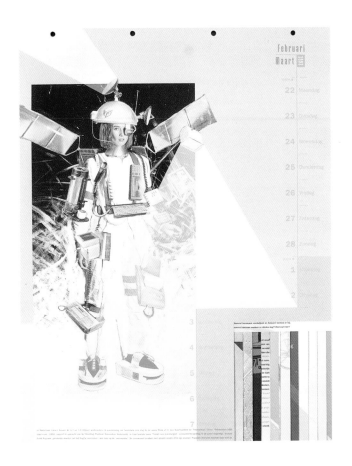

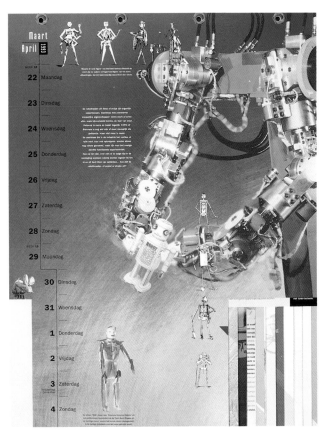

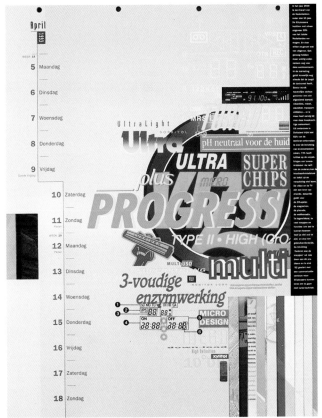

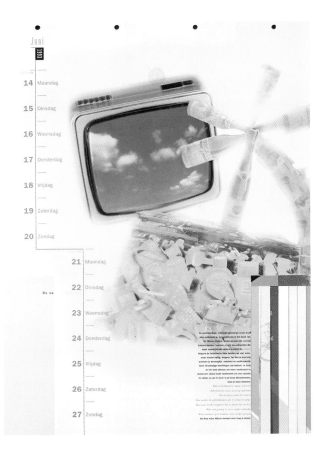

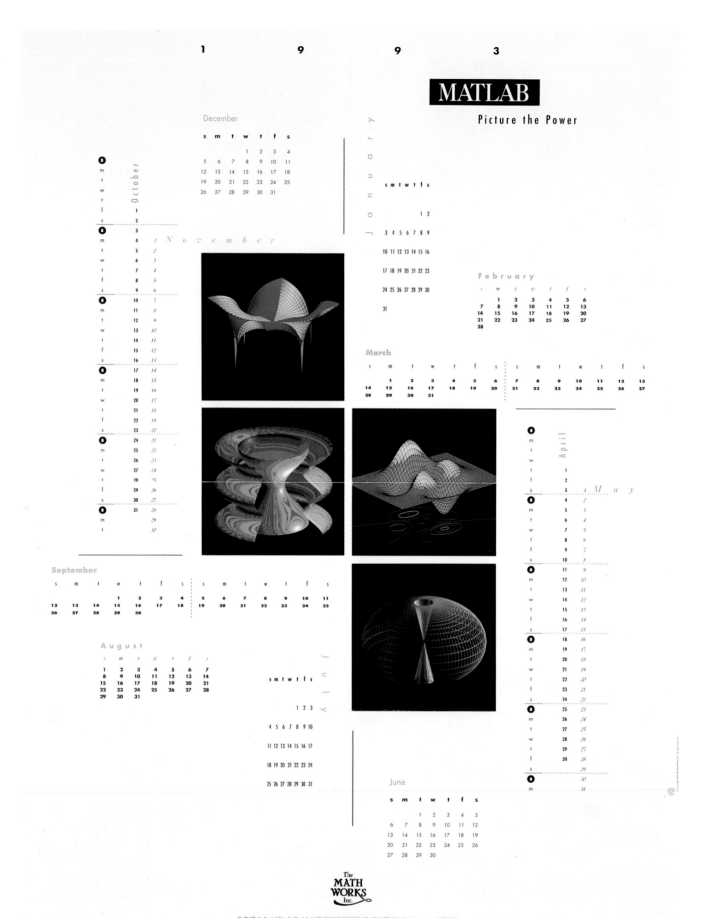

The Mathworks, Inc.

Computer software developer / For promotional purposes
コンピュータ ソフトウェア開発 / プロモーション　USA　1993
CD: Kathleen Forsythe　D: Joan Bitiner　DF: Forsythe Design
size 685×913 mm

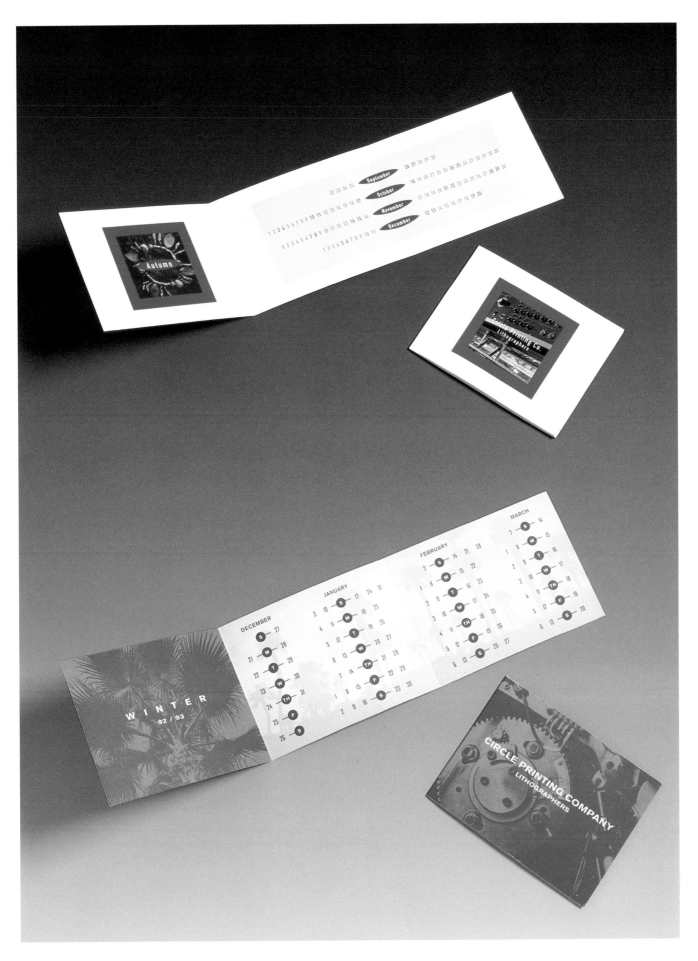

Circle Printing Company

Printing company / For promotional purposes　印刷／プロモーション　USA　1992 1993
CD, AD, D, CW: Eric Ruffing　P: Mary Wilson　DF: 13th Floor　size 180×415 mm

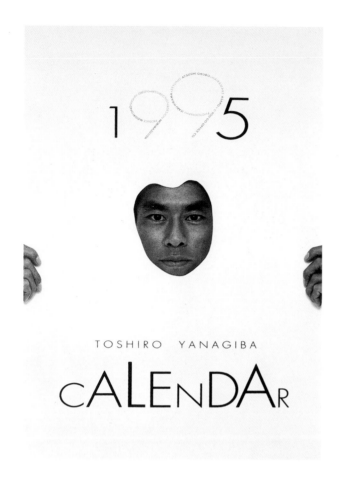

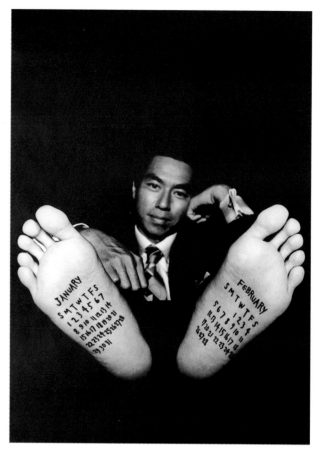

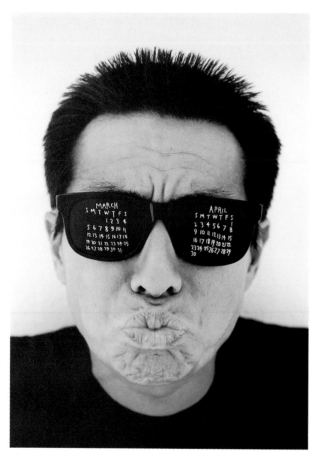

You Go Office Co., Ltd.　㈱融合事務所

Artist management / For retail sales　タレント プロダクション／市販品　Japan 1995
CD, AD, D: Nobukazu Iida　P: Itaru Hirama　Model: Toshiro Yanagiba　DF: Gaga Design Works Inc.
size 515×364 mm

august

andré thijssen

sunday/zondag	15
monday/maandag	16
tuesday/dinsdag	17
wednesday/woensdag	18
thursday/donderdag	19
friday/vrijdag	20
saturday/zaterdag	21

september andré thijssen

| sunday zondag 5 | monday maandag 6 | tuesday dinsdag 7 | wednesday woensdag 8 | thursday donderdag 9 | friday vrijdag 10 | saturday zaterdag 11 |

augustus

drukkerij mart. spruijt bv

drukkerij mart. spruijt bv september

Drunkkerij Mart. Spruijt bv

Printing company / For promotional purposes　印刷 / プロモーション　Netherlands　1993
CD, AD: André Toet　D: Paul Chessel　P: André Thijssen　CW: Jan Kohlmann / John Thacakara
DF: Samenwerkende Ontwerpers bv　size 330×330 mm

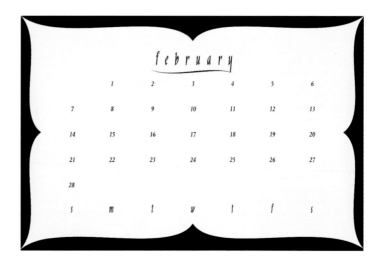

Westland Graphics

Printing company / For promotional purposes　印刷／プロモーション　USA　1993
CD: Marcia Mosko　AD, D, I: Margo Chase　DF: Margo Chase Design　size 700×970 mm

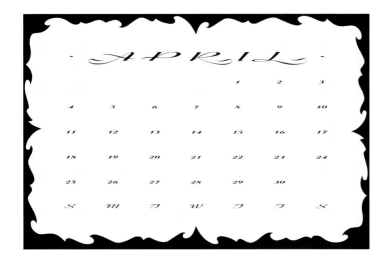

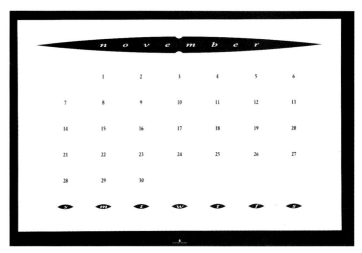

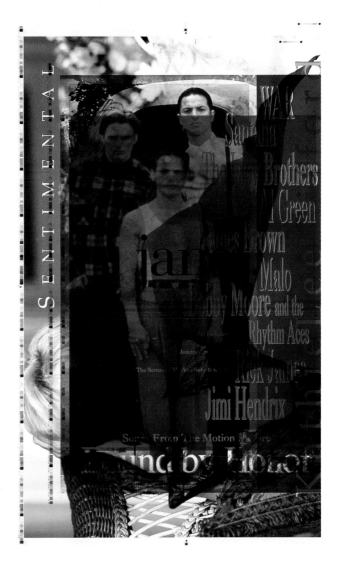

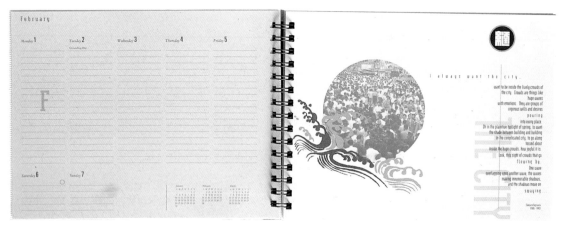

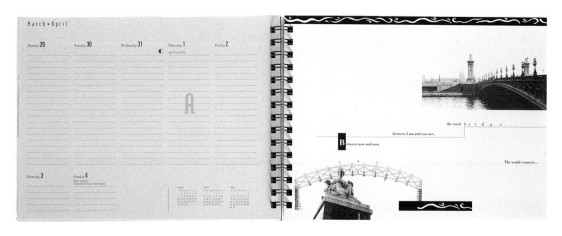

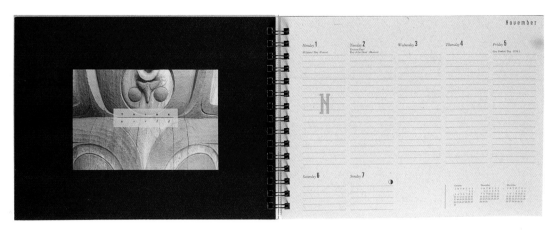

NBBJ

Architects office / For promotional purposes　建築会社 / プロモーション　USA 1993
AD: Kerry Burg　D: Joe Cachero / Susan Dewey　D, P: Stefanie Choi / Doug Keyes / Margo Sepanski
D, P, I: Klindt Parker　P: Julia Russell　I: Brent Rogers　CW: Anita Carmin-Tomisser
DF: NBBJ Graphic Design　size 210×280 mm

MILLENOVECENTO **NOVANTATRE**

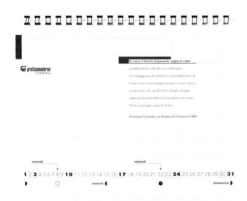

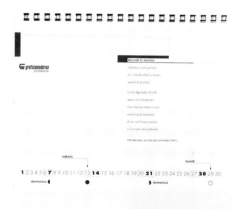

gennaio

maggio

novembre

Grafica Moderna

Printing company / For promotional purposes　印刷／プロモーション　Italy 1994
CD, AD, D, CW: Renato Alongi　P: Alessandro Alongi / Fabio Marino / Nicola Gucciardi
DF: Renato Alongi Graphic Design　size 305×325 mm

Fachhochschule Wiesbaden

College of design / For promotional purposes デザイン学校／プロモーション Germany 1993
CD, AD, D: Klaus Bietz   P: students of Fachhochschule Wiesbaden   size 600×800 mm

1 9 9 5

maart

Lente maand

april

Hooi*maand*

3
4 11 18 25
5 12 19 26
6 13 20 27
7 14 21 28
1 8 15 22 29
2 9 16 23
30

10 17 24 31

4 11 18 25
5 12 19 26
6 13 20 27
7 14 21 28
1 8 15 22 29
2 9 16 23 30
3 10 17 24 31

Winter*maand*

december

At R.e.s. we respond quickly and easily to the challenges of change. Some companies can be so big they're muscle-bound, or so bureaucratic they're hidebound: but the readiness to act with initiative and flexibility runs throughout all levels of our organisation, from getting messages through to getting things done.

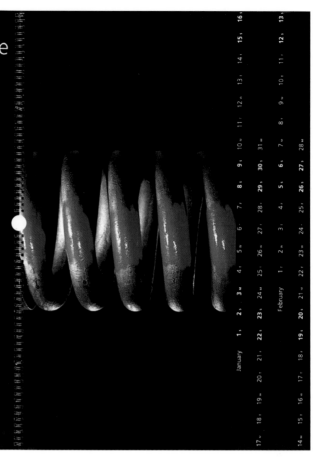

R.e.s. is more than a network of trains, terminals and technology. We're a network of humanity, too: a tight knit team of people. Planners, marshallers, managers, drivers, engineers, R.e.s. people, Royal Mail and other British Rail people, all forging the working relationship we need to make sure the mail gets through.

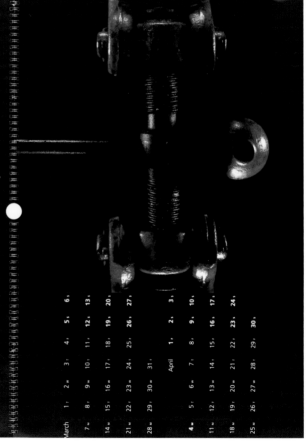

Rail Express Systems

Rail freight company / For promotional purposes　鉄道貨物サービス / プロモーション　England 1994
CD: Nancy Williams / Phoa Kia Boon　AD: Sarah Jane McKenzie　D: Tim Beard / Tim Webb Jenkins
P: Richard Dean / Richard Burbridge　CW: Gordon Fielding　DF: Williams and Phoa
size 600×410 mm

There is no real way to measure the integrity, dedication, honesty and professional pride that keep us fit to face the challenges of today's modern light freight business. There are only 600 people in the whole of R.e.s.: but just imagine the total years of experience, skill and expertise behind that tightly knit team.

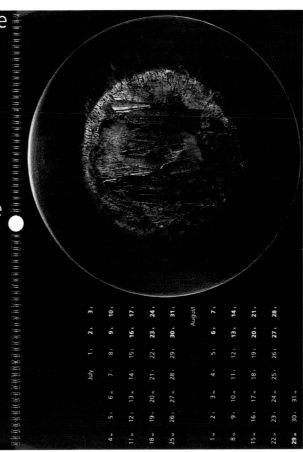

R.e.s. and Royal Mail together are investing around £120 million in new trains, terminals and technology. This investment isn't simply for the sake of innovation; it's to help us to grow and expand, so that we can continue to deliver specific customer benefits, such as speed and efficiency.

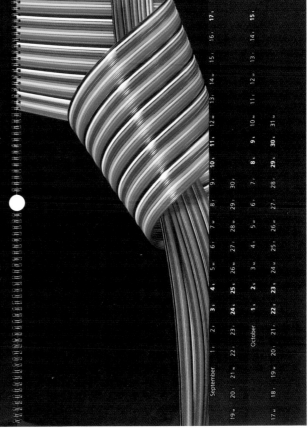

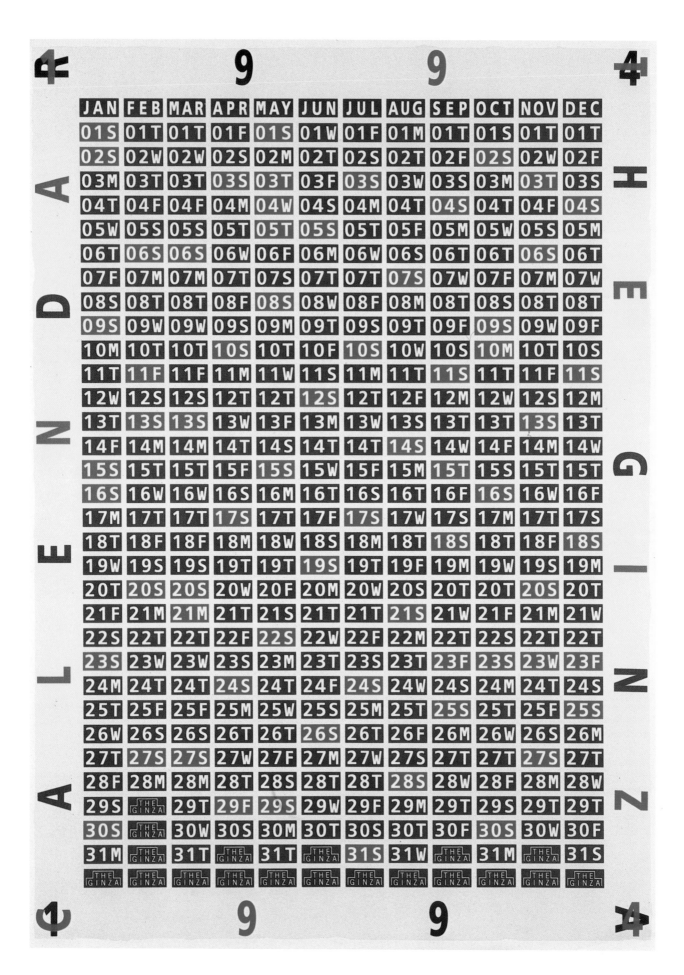

The Ginza Co., Ltd. ㈱ ザ ギンザ

Boutique / For promotional purposes　ブティック / プロモーション　Japan 1994
CD: Katsumi Yamada　AD, D: Masayoshi Nakajo　size 1030×730 mm

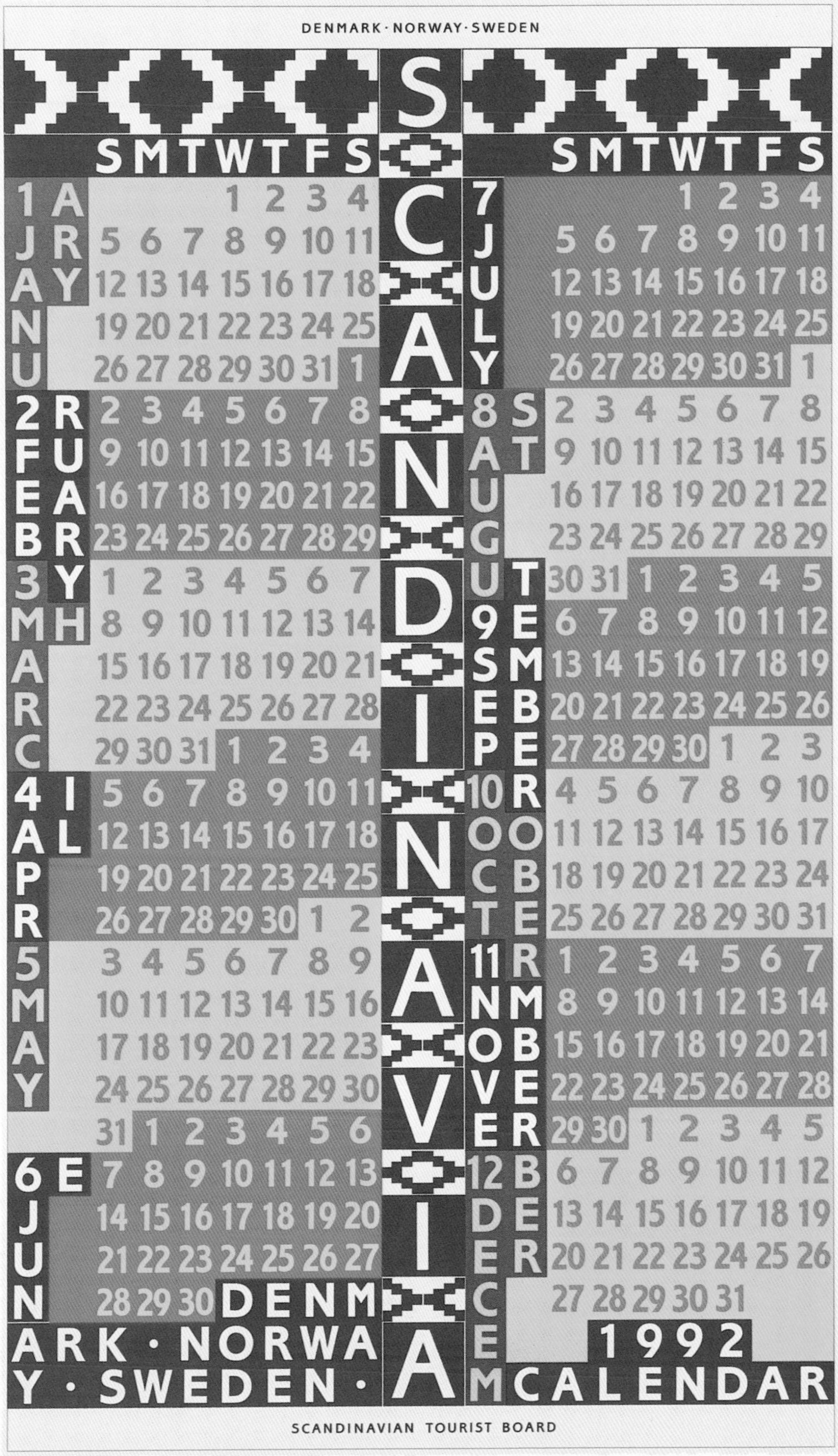

DENMARK · NORWAY · SWEDEN

SCANDINAVIA

DENMARK · NORWAY · SWEDEN · SCANDINAVIA

1992 CALENDAR

SCANDINAVIAN TOURIST BOARD

Scandinavia Tourist Board　スカンジナビア観光局

Tourist office / For promotional purposes　観光局 / プロモーション　Japan 1992
CD: Hiromi Murakami　AD, D: Masayoshi Nakajo　size 1030×660 mm

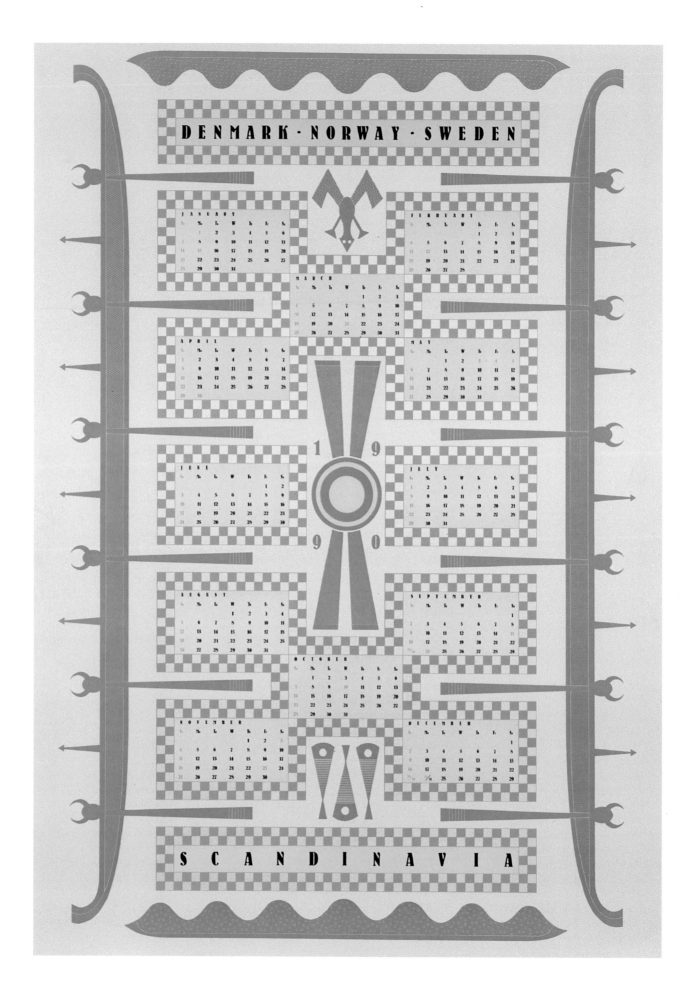

Scandinavia Tourist Board　スカンジナビア観光局

Tourist office / For promotional purposes　観光局／プロモーション　Japan 1990
CD: Hiromi Murakami　AD, D: Masayoshi Nakajo　size 1030×730 mm

S C A N D I N A V I A スカンジア観光局

january

sun	mon	tue	wed	thu	fri	sat
		1	2	3	4	5
6	7	8	9	10	11	12
13	14	15	16	17	18	19
20	21	22	23	24	25	26
27	28	29	30	31		

february

sun	mon	tue	wed	thu	fri	sat
					1	2
3	4	5	6	7	8	9
10	11	12	13	14	15	16
17	18	19	20	21	22	23
24	25	26	27	28		

march

sun	mon	tue	wed	thu	fri	sat
					1	2
3	4	5	6	7	8	9
10	11	12	13	14	15	16
17	18	19	20	21	22	23
24 31	25	26	27	28	29	30

april

sun	mon	tue	wed	thu	fri	sat
	1	2	3	4	5	6
7	8	9	10	11	12	13
14	15	16	17	18	19	20
21	22	23	24	25	26	27
28	29	30				

may

sun	mon	tue	wed	thu	fri	sat
			1	2	3	4
5	6	7	8	9	10	11
12	13	14	15	16	17	18
19	20	21	22	23	24	25
26	27	28	29	30	31	

june

sun	mon	tue	wed	thu	fri	sat
						1
2	3	4	5	6	7	8
9	10	11	12	13	14	15
16	17	18	19	20	21	22
23 30	24	25	26	27	28	29

july

sun	mon	tue	wed	thu	fri	sat
	1	2	3	4	5	6
7	8	9	10	11	12	13
14	15	16	17	18	19	20
21	22	23	24	25	26	27
28	29	30	31			

august

sun	mon	tue	wed	thu	fri	sat
				1	2	3
4	5	6	7	8	9	10
11	12	13	14	15	16	17
18	19	20	21	22	23	24
25	26	27	28	29	30	31

september

sun	mon	tue	wed	thu	fri	sat
1	2	3	4	5	6	7
8	9	10	11	12	13	14
15	16	17	18	19	20	21
22	23	24	25	26	27	28
29	30					

october

sun	mon	tue	wed	thu	fri	sat
		1	2	3	4	5
6	7	8	9	10	11	12
13	14	15	16	17	18	19
20	21	22	23	24	25	26
27	28	29	30	31		

november

sun	mon	tue	wed	thu	fri	sat
					1	2
3	4	5	6	7	8	9
10	11	12	13	14	15	16
17	18	19	20	21	22	23
24	25	26	27	28	29	30

december

sun	mon	tue	wed	thu	fri	sat
1	2	3	4	5	6	7
8	9	10	11	12	13	14
15	16	17	18	19	20	21
22	23	24	25	26	27	28
29	30	31				

C A L E N D A R 1 9 9 1

D E N M A R K · N O R W A Y · S W E D E N

SCANDINAVIAN TOURIST BOARD

Scandinavia Tourist Board スカンジナビア観光局

Tourist office / For promotional purposes　観光局 / プロモーション　Japan　1991
CD: Hiromi Murakami　AD, D: Masayoshi Nakajo　size 1030×730 mm

1993 CALENDAR

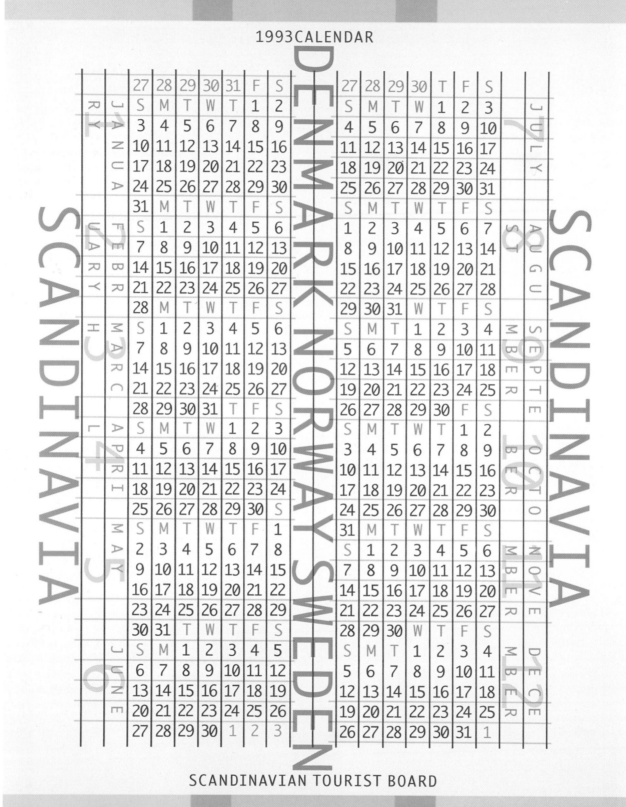

SCANDINAVIAN TOURIST BOARD

Scandinavia Tourist Board　スカンジナビア観光局

Tourist office / For promotional purposes　観光局 / プロモーション　Japan 1993
CD: Hiromi Murakami　AD, D: Masayoshi Nakajo　size 1030×730 mm

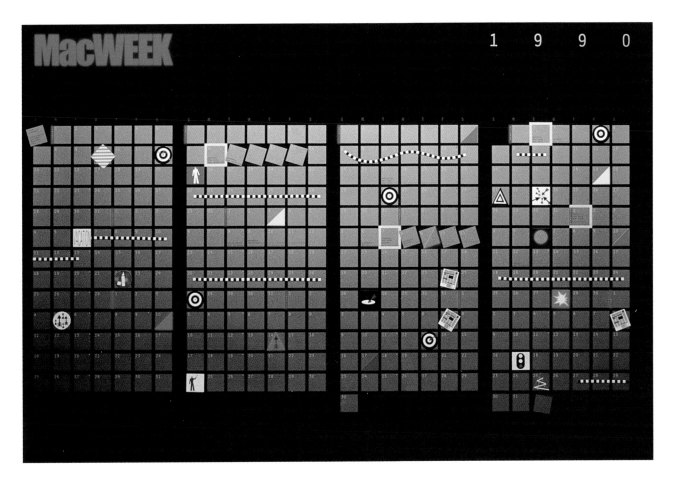

Macweek Magazine

Magazine publisher / For promotional purposes　雑誌出版／プロモーション　USA 1990
CD, D: Mitchell Mauk　DF: Mauk Design　size 598×925 mm

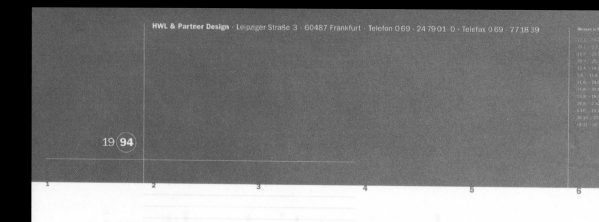

HWL & Partner Design · Leipziger Straße 3 · 60487 Frankfurt · Telefon 0 69 · 24 79 01- 0 · Telefax 0 69 · 77 18 39

19(94)

januar
—

februar
—

märz
—

april
—

mai
—

juni
—

HWL & Partner Design

Graphic design firm / For promotional purposes　グラフィック デザイン / プロモーション
Germany 1994   CD, AD, D: Klaus Bietz   DF: HWL & Partner Design   size 800×500 mm

In Hessen

1./3.94 · Weihnachtsferien
5.4.94 · Osterferien
·5.5.94 · Pfingstferien
8.6.94 · Sommerferien
26.10.94 · Herbstferien
11.1.95 · Weihnachtsferien

Die Typografie ist in gewisser Weise vergleichbar
mit dem Licht – sie kann völlig transparent sein.
Sie birgt in sich den sublimen Widerspruch gleichzeitig
schön und unsichtbar zu sein.
Zum größten Teil der Zeit wird sie für die meisten Menschen
als etwas Selbstverständliches hingenommen –
so wie auch unsere natürliche Umgebung.
Das liegt – glaube ich – daran, daß unser Leben mit Typografie überläuft,
und die Typografie somit zu einem vorausgesetzten Hintergrund
unserer visuellen Landschaft wurde.

Hitoshi Koizumi

8   9   10   11   12

august

	29
1	Mo
2	Di
3	Mi
4	Do
5	Fr
6	Sa
7	So
8	Mo
9	Di
10	Mi
11	Do
12	Fr
13	Sa
14	So
15	Mo
16	Di
17	Mi
18	Do
19	Fr
20	Sa
21	So
22	Mo
23	Di
24	Mi
25	Fr
26	Fr
27	Sa
28	So
29	Mo
30	Di
31	Mi

september

1	Do
2	Fr
3	Sa
4	So
5	Mo
6	Di
7	Mi
8	Do
9	Fr
10	Sa
11	So
12	Mo
13	Di
14	Mi
15	Do
16	Fr
17	Sa
18	So
19	Mo
20	Di
21	Mi
22	Do
23	Fr
24	Sa
25	So
26	Mo
27	Di
28	Mi
29	Do
30	Fr

oktober

1	Sa
2	So
3	Mo
4	Di
5	Mi
6	Do
7	Fr
8	Sa
9	So
10	Mo
11	Di
12	Mi
13	Do
14	Fr
15	Sa
16	So
17	Mo
18	Di
19	Mi
20	Do
21	Fr
22	Sa
23	So
24	Mo
25	Di
26	Mi
27	Do
28	Fr
29	Sa
30	So
31	Mo

november

1	Di
2	Mi
3	Do
4	Fr
5	Sa
6	So
7	Mo
8	Di
9	Mi
10	Do
11	Fr
12	Sa
13	So
14	Mo
15	Di
16	Mi
17	Do
18	Fr
19	Sa
20	So
21	Mo
22	Di
23	Mi
24	Do
25	Fr
26	Sa
27	So
28	Mo
29	Di
30	Mi

dezember

1	Do
2	Fr
3	Sa
4	So
5	Mo
6	Di
7	Mi
8	Do
9	Fr
10	Sa
11	So
12	Mo
13	Di
14	Mi
15	Do
16	Fr
17	Sa
18	So
19	Mo
20	Di
21	Mi
22	Do
23	Fr
24	Sa
25	So
26	Mo
27	Di
28	Mi
29	Do
30	Fr
31	Sa

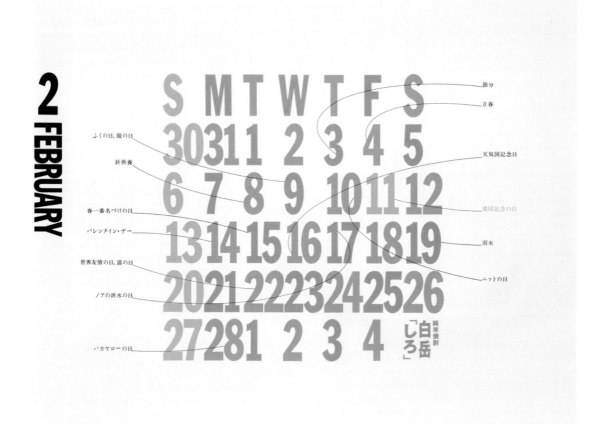

Takahashi Shuzoh （合）高橋酒造本店

Liquor manufacturer / For promotional purposes　酒造／プロモーション　Japan 1994
AD: Kazuya Takaoka　D: Harumi Asao　CW: Ben Uozumi　DF: DK Co., Ltd.　size 365×450 mm

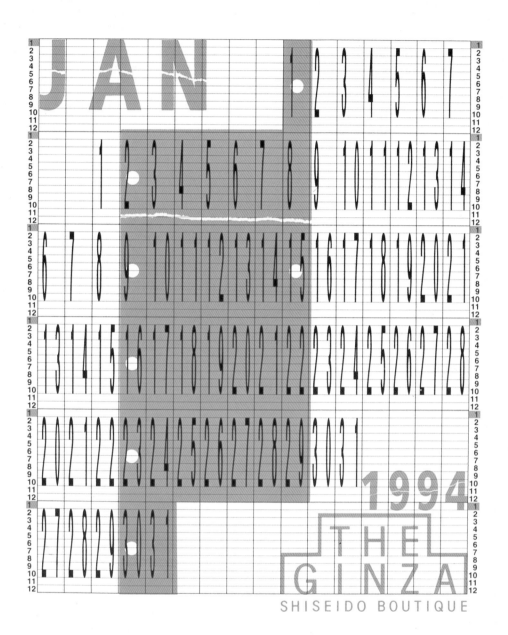

The Ginza Co., Ltd. ㈱ ザ ギンザ

Boutique / For promotional purposes　ブティック / プロモーション　Japan 1994
CD: Katsumi Yamada　AD, D: Masayoshi Nakajo　size 620×510 mm

January 1

1 2 3 4 5 6 7 8 9 10 11 12 13 14 15 16 17 18 19 20 21 22 23 24 25 26 27 28 29 30 31

February 2

1 2 3 4 5 6 7 8 9 10 11 12 13 14 15 16 17 18 19 20 21 22 23 24 25 26 27 28

March 3

1 2 3 4 5 6 7 8 9 10 11 12 13 14 15 16 17 18 19 20 21 22 23 24 25 26 27 28 29 30 31

April 4

1 2 3 4 5 6 7 8 9 10 11 12 13 14 15 16 17 18 19 20 21 22 23 24 25 26 27 28 29 30

May 5

1 2 3 4 5 6 7 8 9 10 11 12 13 14 15 16 17 18 19 20 21 22 23 24 25 26 27 28 29 30 31

June 6

1 2 3 4 5 6 7 8 9 10 11 12 13 14 15 16 17 18 19 20 21 22 23 24 25 26 27 28 29 30

July 7

1 2 3 4 5 6 7 8 9 10 11 12 13 14 15 16 17 18 19 20 21 22 23 24 25 26 27 28 29 30 31

August 8

1 2 3 4 5 6 7 8 9 10 11 12 13 14 15 16 17 18 19 20 21 22 23 24 25 26 27 28 29 30 31

September 9

1 2 3 4 5 6 7 8 9 10 11 12 13 14 15 16 17 18 19 20 21 22 23 24 25 26 27 28 29 30

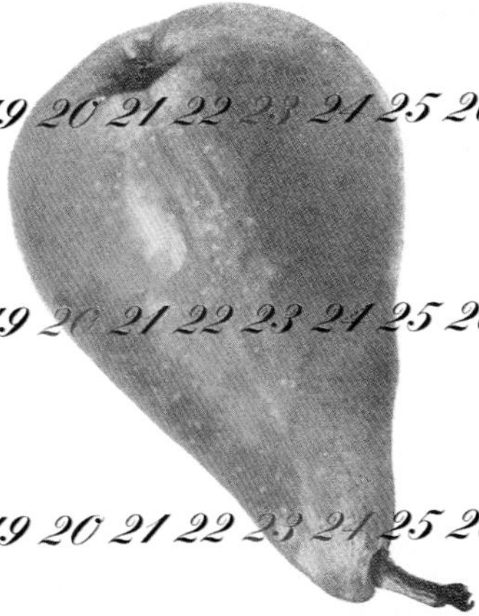

October 10

1 2 3 4 5 6 7 8 9 10 11 12 13 14 15 16 17 18 19 20 21 22 23 24 25 26 27 28 29 30 31

November 11

1 2 3 4 5 6 7 8 9 10 11 12 13 14 15 16 17 18 19 20 21 22 23 24 25 26 27 28 29 30

December 12

1 2 3 4 5 6 7 8 9 10 11 12 13 14 15 16 17 18 19 20 21 22 23 24 25 26 27 28 29 30 31

The Emerald Isle

1994

Importers and Wholesalers of fine-quality gemstones.
The superior source for all types of loose stones.
1 800 88 EMERALD

Months (diagonal labels): JANUARY, FEBRUARY, MARCH, APRIL, MAY, JUNE, JULY, AUGUST, SEPTEMBER, OCTOBER, NOVEMBER, DECEMBER

Birthstones:
- Birthstone: Garnet (January)
- Birthstone: Amethyst (February)
- Birthstone: Aquamarine or Bloodstone (March)
- Birthstone: Diamond (April)
- Birthstone: Emerald (May)
- Birthstone: Pearl, Moonstone or Alexandrite (June)
- Birthstone: Ruby (July)
- Birthstone: Peridot (August)
- Birthstone: Sapphire (September)
- Birthstone: Opal or Tourmaline (October)
- Birthstone: Topaz or Citrine (November)
- Birthstone: Turquoise or Zircon (December)

The Emerald Isle / P.O. Box 1859 / Boston, Massachusetts 02205 / Phone: 1 800 88 EMERALD / 508 651 3153 / Fax: 508 651 3133

The Emerald Isle

Gemstone importer / For promotional purposes 宝石輸入・卸売 / プロモーション USA 1994
CD, AD, D, I, CW: Theodore Groves size 280×433 mm

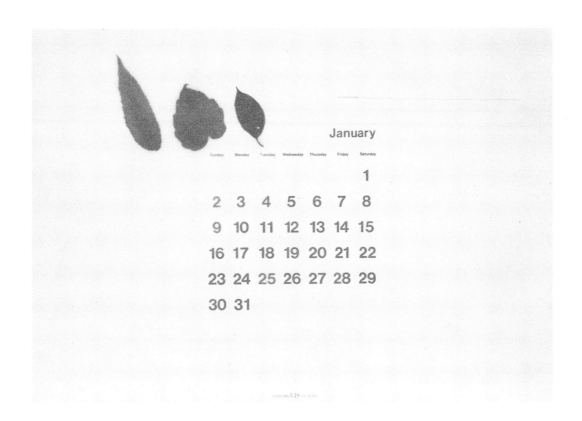

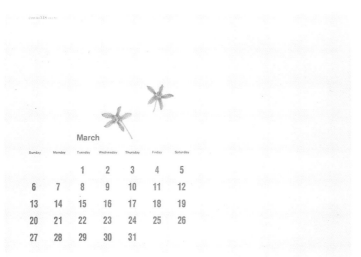

Studio VIS Co., Ltd.　㈱ スタジオ ビス

Graphic design firm / For private use　グラフィック デザイン / プライベート　Japan　1995
CD, AD: Koji Kusatsugu　D: Kyoko Izumi / Tetsuya Takeuchi / Masae Kono　DF: Studio VIS Co., Ltd.
size 257×364 mm

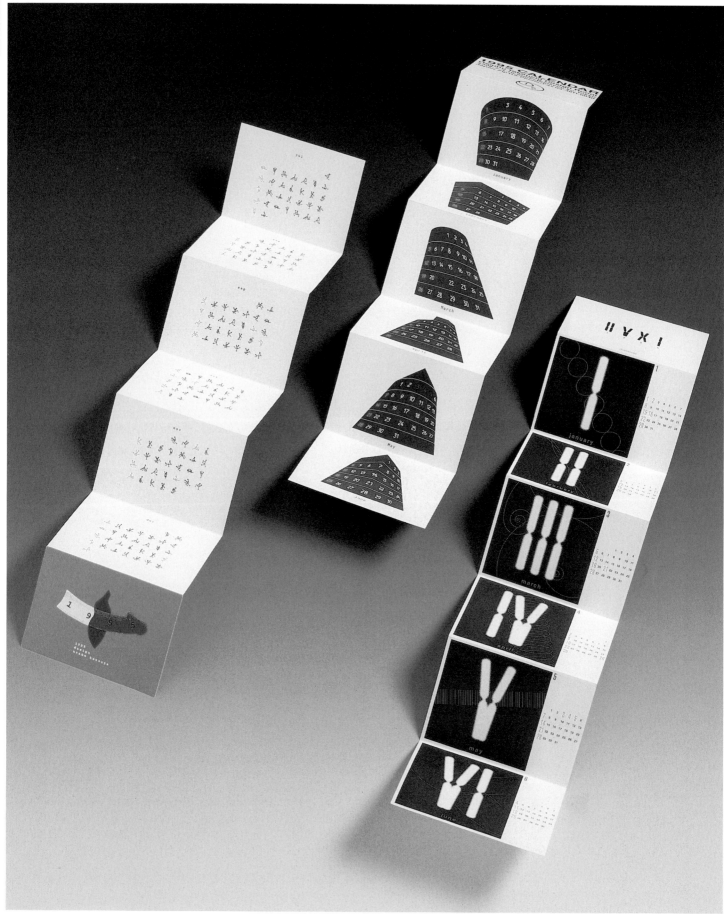

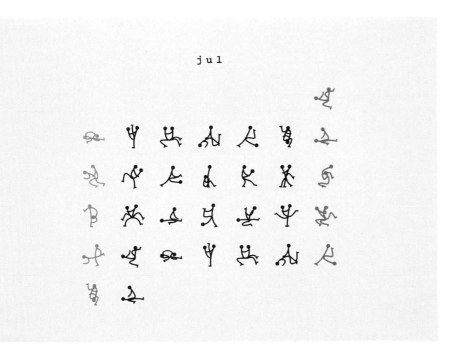

Katsuya Urabe   占部克也

Graphic designer / For private use
グラフィック デザイン / プライベート   Japan 1995
CD, AD, D, I: Katsuya Urabe   size 725×147 mm

Osamu Takeuchi Design Room   竹内オサム デザイン室

Graphic design & advertising / For promotional purposes
グラフィック デザイン・広告制作 / プロモーション   Japan 1995
CD, AD, D: Osamu Takeuchi   D: Kenji Nakato
DF: Osamu Takeuchi Design Room   size 725×147 mm

Creators Group MAC   クリエイターズグループ MAC

Graphic design & advertising / For promotional purposes
グラフィック デザイン・広告制作 / プロモーション   Japan 1995
CD, AD, D: Akio Kenmochi   DF: Creators Group MAC   size 725×147 mm

A P R I L

APRIL

A V R I L

MO   DI   MI   DO   FR   SA   SO

				1	13		**2**	**3**
4	5	6	7	8	14		9	**10**
11	12	13	14	15	15		16	**17**
18	19	20	21	22	16		23	**24**
25	26	27	28	29	17		30	

MO   TU   WE   TH   FR   SA   SU

LU   MA   ME   JE   VE   SA   DI

GEBR SCHMIDT
DRUCKFARBEN

Gebr. Schmidt Druckfarben

Printing ink manufacturer / For promotional purposes   印刷用インク メーカー / プロモーション
Germany 1994   CD, AD, D: Fritz Hofrichter   D: Heike Messerschmitt   P: Alexander Geibel
CW: Eda Weiss   DF: HWL & Partner Design   size 390×560 mm

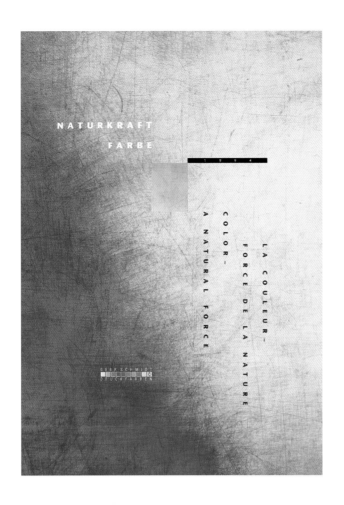

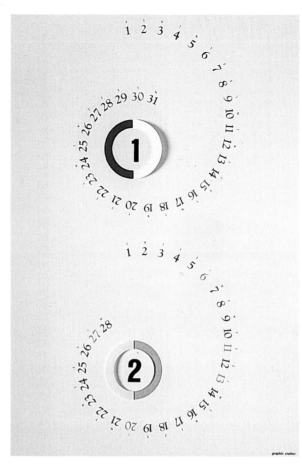

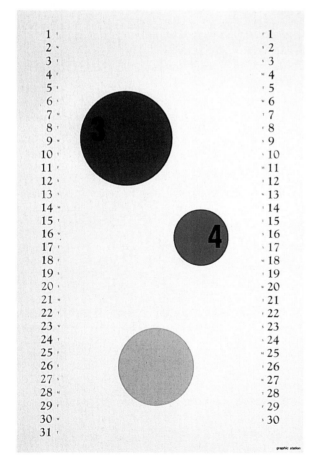

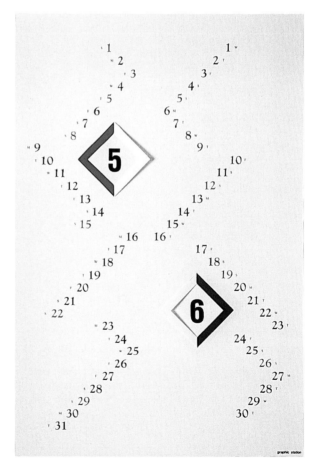

Art Print Japan Co., Ltd. ㈱ アートプリントジャパン

Stationery supplier / For retail sales　ポスター、カード製造・販売 / 市販品　Japan　1994
BR: graphic station　D: Mutsuko Morita　size 390×255 mm

graphik calender 94 by wolf wopmann

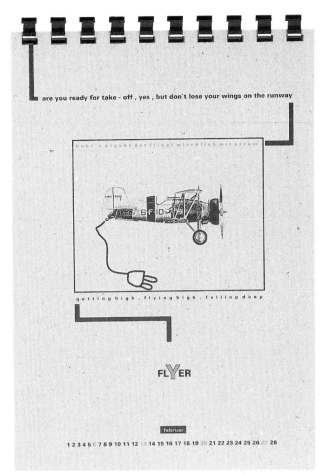

are you ready for take - off , yes , but don`t lose your wings on the runway

getting high , flying high , falling deep

FLYER

februar

1 2 3 4 5 6 7 8 9 10 11 12 13 14 15 16 17 18 19 20 21 22 23 24 25 26 27 28

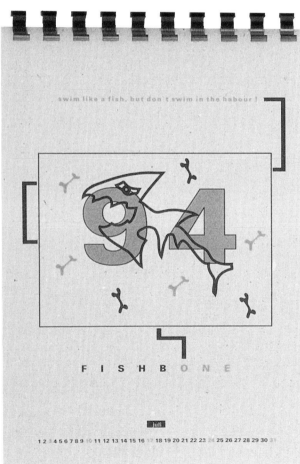

swim like a fish, but don`t swim in the habour !

F I S H B O N E

juli

1 2 3 4 5 6 7 8 9 10 11 12 13 14 15 16 17 18 19 20 21 22 23 24 25 26 27 28 29 30 31

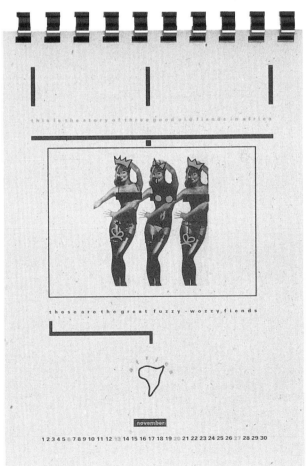

this is the story of three good old fiends in africa

these are the great fuzzy - wozzy , fiends

november

1 2 3 4 5 6 7 8 9 10 11 12 13 14 15 16 17 18 19 20 21 22 23 24 25 26 27 28 29 30

Wolf Wopmann

Graphic designer / For private use　グラフィック デザイン / プライベート　Austria　1994
D, I: Wolf Wopmann　size 210×148 mm

1995

	1 JANUARY JANVIER	2 FEBRUARY FEVRIER	3 MARCH MARS	4 APRIL AVRIL	5 MAY MAI	6 JUNE JUIN	7 JULY JUILLET	8 AUGUST AOUT	9 SEPTEMBER SEPTEMBRE	10 OCTOBER OCTOBRE	11 NOVEMBER NOVEMBRE	12 DECEMBER DECEMBRE
MONDAY LUNDI					1							
TUESDAY MARDI					2			1				
WEDNESDAY MERCREDI		1	1		3			2			1	
THURSDAY JEUDI		2	2		4	1		3			2	
FRIDAY VENDREDI		3	3		5	2		4	1		3	1
SATURDAY SAMEDI		4	4	1	6	3	1	5	2		4	2
SUNDAY DIMANCHE	1	5	5	2	7	4	2	6	3	1	5	3
MONDAY LUNDI	2	6	6	3	8	5	3	7	4	2	6	4
TUESDAY MARDI	3	7	7	4	9	6	4	8	5	3	7	5
WEDNESDAY MERCREDI	4	8	8	5	10	7	5	9	6	4	8	6
THURSDAY JEUDI	5	9	9	6	11	8	6	10	7	5	9	7
FRIDAY VENDREDI	6	10	10	7	12	9	7	11	8	6	10	8
SATURDAY SAMEDI	7	11	11	8	13	10	8	12	9	7	11	9
SUNDAY DIMANCHE	8	12	12	9	14	11	9	13	10	8	12	10
MONDAY LUNDI	9	13	13	10	15	12	10	14	11	9	13	11
TUESDAY MARDI	10	14	14	11	16	13	11	15	12	10	14	12
WEDNESDAY MERCREDI	11	15	15	12	17	14	12	16	13	11	15	13
THURSDAY JEUDI	12	16	16	13	18	15	13	17	14	12	16	14
FRIDAY VENDREDI	13	17	17	14	19	16	14	18	15	13	17	15
SATURDAY SAMEDI	14	18	18	15	20	17	15	19	16	14	18	16
SUNDAY DIMANCHE	15	19	19	16	21	18	16	20	17	15	19	17
MONDAY LUNDI	16	20	20	17	22	19	17	21	18	16	20	18
TUESDAY MARDI	17	21	21	18	23	20	18	22	19	17	21	19
WEDNESDAY MERCREDI	18	22	22	19	24	21	19	23	20	18	22	20
THURSDAY JEUDI	19	23	23	20	25	22	20	24	21	19	23	21
FRIDAY VENDREDI	20	24	24	21	26	23	21	25	22	20	24	22
SATURDAY SAMEDI	21	25	25	22	27	24	22	26	23	21	25	23
SUNDAY DIMANCHE	22	26	26	23	28	25	23	27	24	22	26	24
MONDAY LUNDI	23	27	27	24	29	26	24	28	25	23	27	25
TUESDAY MARDI	24	28	28	25	30	27	25	29	26	24	28	26
WEDNESDAY MERCREDI	25		29	26	31	28	26	30	27	25	29	27
THURSDAY JEUDI	26		30	27		29	27	31	28	26	30	28
FRIDAY VENDREDI	27		31	28		30	28		29	27		29
SATURDAY SAMEDI	28			29			29		30	28		30
SUNDAY DIMANCHE	29			30			30			29		31
MONDAY LUNDI	30						31			30		
TUESDAY MARDI	31									31		

etranger di costarica corporation ㈲エトランジェ ディ コスタリカ

Stationery supplier / For retail sales　雑貨、ステーショナリー企画製作 / 市販品　Japan 1995
AD, D: Hiroshi Murakami　size 594×420 mm

ALL THE PEOPLE LOVES OUR SOCKS

100% HOME MADE SOCKS
靴下屋
PRODUCED BY
DAN CO., LTD.

CALENDAR 1995

WE SUPPORT YOUR SOCKS LIFE

1 January

Sun	Mon	Tue	Wed	Thu	Fri	Sat
1	2	3	4	5	6	7
8	9	10	11	12	13	14
15	16	17	18	19	20	21
22	23	24	25	26	27	28
29	30	31				

2 February

Sun	Mon	Tue	Wed	Thu	Fri	Sat
			1	2	3	4
5	6	7	8	9	10	11
12	13	14	15	16	17	18
19	20	21	22	23	24	25
26	27	28				

3 March

Sun	Mon	Tue	Wed	Thu	Fri	Sat
			1	2	3	4
5	6	7	8	9	10	11
12	13	14	15	16	17	18
19	20	21	22	23	24	25
26	27	28	29	30	31	

4 April

Sun	Mon	Tue	Wed	Thu	Fri	Sat
						1
2	3	4	5	6	7	8
9	10	11	12	13	14	15
16	17	18	19	20	21	22
23/30	24	25	26	27	28	29

5 May

Sun	Mon	Tue	Wed	Thu	Fri	Sat
	1	2	3	4	5	6
7	8	9	10	11	12	13
14	15	16	17	18	19	20
21	22	23	24	25	26	27
28	29	30	31			

6 June

Sun	Mon	Tue	Wed	Thu	Fri	Sat
				1	2	3
4	5	6	7	8	9	10
11	12	13	14	15	16	17
18	19	20	21	22	23	24
25	26	27	28	29	30	

7 July

Sun	Mon	Tue	Wed	Thu	Fri	Sat
						1
2	3	4	5	6	7	8
9	10	11	12	13	14	15
16	17	18	19	20	21	22
23/30	24/31	25	26	27	28	29

8 August

Sun	Mon	Tue	Wed	Thu	Fri	Sat
		1	2	3	4	5
6	7	8	9	10	11	12
13	14	15	16	17	18	19
20	21	22	23	24	25	26
27	28	29	30	31		

9 September

Sun	Mon	Tue	Wed	Thu	Fri	Sat
					1	2
3	4	5	6	7	8	9
10	11	12	13	14	15	16
17	18	19	20	21	22	23
24	25	26	27	28	29	30

10 October

Sun	Mon	Tue	Wed	Thu	Fri	Sat
1	2	3	4	5	6	7
8	9	10	11	12	13	14
15	16	17	18	19	20	21
22	23	24	25	26	27	28
29	30	31				

11 November

Sun	Mon	Tue	Wed	Thu	Fri	Sat
			1	2	3	4
5	6	7	8	9	10	11
12	13	14	15	16	17	18
19	20	21	22	23	24	25
26	27	28	29	30		

12 December

Sun	Mon	Tue	Wed	Thu	Fri	Sat
					1	2
3	4	5	6	7	8	9
10	11	12	13	14	15	16
17	18	19	20	21	22	23
24/31	25	26	27	28	29	30

Dan Co., Ltd.　㈱ ダン

Sock manufacturer / For promotional purposes　靴下メーカー / プロモーション　Japan 1995
BR: Kutsushitaya　size 515×325 mm

1995

*

Origina

lendar

*

1995

Original

Calendar

*

1995 January 1	December '94	1995 2 February	March 1995 3
	31		31
	30		30
	29		29
	28	28	28
	27	27	27
	26	26	26
	25	25	25
	24	24	24
	23	23	23
	22	22	22
	21	21	21
	20	20	20
	19	19	19
	18	18	18
	17	17	17
	16	16	16
	15	15	15
	14	14	14
	13	13	13
	12	12	12
	11	11	11
	10	10	10
	9	9	9
	8	8	8
	7	7	7
	6	6	6
	5	5	5
	4	4	4
	3	3	3
	2	2	2
	1	1	1

Gallery Interform

Gallery Interform ギャラリーインターフォーム

Stationery supplier / For retail sales
カード、カレンダー製作・販売／市販品　Japan 1995
CD: Masaya Yamaguchi　AD, D: Jun Sato
DF: Jun Sato Design Inc.　size 880×96 mm

Takushoku University   拓殖大学

University / For promotional purposes   大学 / プロモーション   Japan 1994
AD, D: Shoji Koide   size 890×110 mm

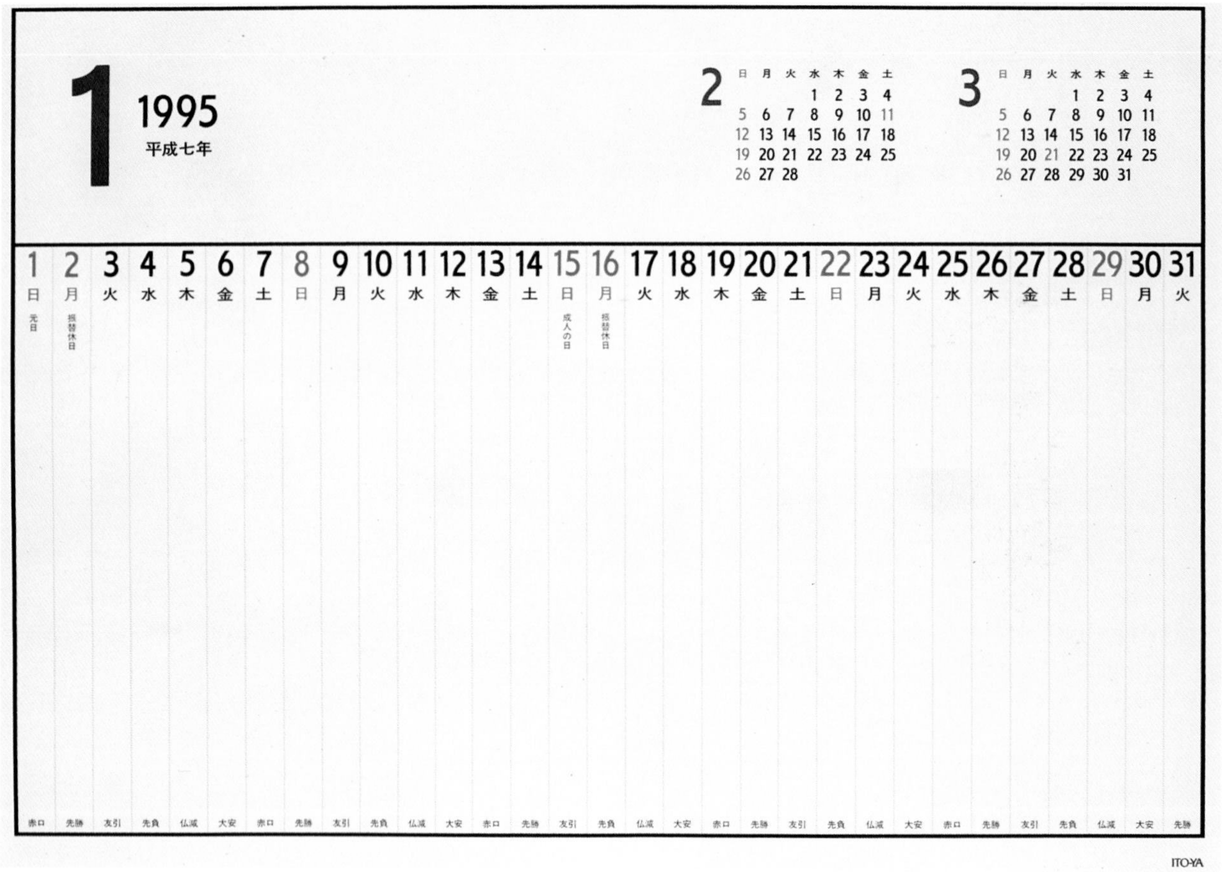

❶

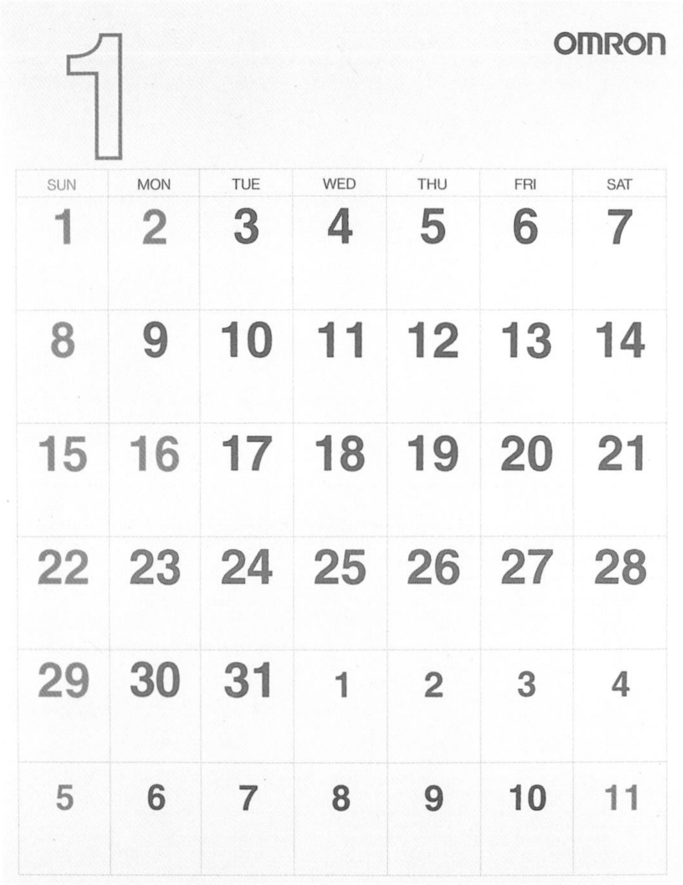

❷

❶
Ito-ya Co., Ltd.　㈱伊東屋

Stationery & art supplies retailer / For retail sales　文具、画材販売 / 市販品　Japan　1995
CD, AD: Takayuki Ito　DF: Ito-ya Product Design Department　size 366×515 mm

❷
Omron Corporation　オムロン㈱

Electronic control equipment manufacturer / For promotional purposes
制御機器メーカー / プロモーション　Japan　1995
CD: Toyoshige Tanaka　AD: Kenji Yoshida　D: Sachiko Saito
DF: CYBAC Co., Ltd.　size 650×518 mm

1993	1	JANUARY				
sun	mon	tue	wed	thu	fri	sat
					1	2
3	4	5	6	7	8	9
10	11	12	13	14	15	16
17	18	19	20	21	22	23
24/31	25	26	27	28	29	30

1993	2	FEBRUARY				
sun	mon	tue	wed	thu	fri	sat
	1	2	3	4	5	6
7	8	9	10	11	12	13
14	15	16	17	18	19	20
21	22	23	24	25	26	27
28						

1993	3	MARCH				
sun	mon	tue	wed	thu	fri	sat
	1	2	3	4	5	6
7	8	9	10	11	12	13
14	15	16	17	18	19	20
21	22	23	24	25	26	27
28	29	30	31			

Calendar

1992	12	DECEMBER				
sun	mon	tue	wed	thu	fri	sat
		1	2	3	4	5
6	7	8	9	10	11	12
13	14	15	16	17	18	19
20	21	22	23	24	25	26
27	28	29	30	31		

SAZABY'S
FURNITURE

1993	4	APRIL				
sun	mon	tue	wed	thu	fri	sat
				1	2	3
4	5	6	7	8	9	10
11	12	13	14	15	16	17
18	19	20	21	22	23	24
25	26	27	28	29	30	

1993	5	MAY				
sun	mon	tue	wed	thu	fri	sat
						1
2	3	4	5	6	7	8
9	10	11	12	13	14	15
16	17	18	19	20	21	22
23/30	24/31	25	26	27	28	29

1993	6	JUNE				
sun	mon	tue	wed	thu	fri	sat
		1	2	3	4	5
6	7	8	9	10	11	12
13	14	15	16	17	18	19
20	21	22	23	24	25	26
27	28	29	30			

1993	7	JULY				
sun	mon	tue	wed	thu	fri	sat
				1	2	3
4	5	6	7	8	9	10
11	12	13	14	15	16	17
18	19	20	21	22	23	24
25	26	27	28	29	30	31

1993	8	AUGUST				
sun	mon	tue	wed	thu	fri	sat
1	2	3	4	5	6	7
8	9	10	11	12	13	14
15	16	17	18	19	20	21
22	23	24	25	26	27	28
29	30	31				

1993	9	SEPTEMBER				
sun	mon	tue	wed	thu	fri	sat
			1	2	3	4
5	6	7	8	9	10	11
12	13	14	15	16	17	18
19	20	21	22	23	24	25
26	27	28	29	30		

Calendar

1994	1	JANUARY				
sun	mon	tue	wed	thu	fri	sat
						1
2	3	4	5	6	7	8
9	10	11	12	13	14	15
16	17	18	19	20	21	22
23/30	24/31	25	26	27	28	29

SAZABY'S
FURNITURE

1993	10	OCTOBER				
sun	mon	tue	wed	thu	fri	sat
					1	2
3	4	5	6	7	8	9
10	11	12	13	14	15	16
17	18	19	20	21	22	23
24/31	25	26	27	28	29	30

1993	11	NOVEMBER				
sun	mon	tue	wed	thu	fri	sat
	1	2	3	4	5	6
7	8	9	10	11	12	13
14	15	16	17	18	19	20
21	22	23	24	25	26	27
28	29	30				

1993	12	DECEMBER				
sun	mon	tue	wed	thu	fri	sat
			1	2	3	4
5	6	7	8	9	10	11
12	13	14	15	16	17	18
19	20	21	22	23	24	25
26	27	28	29	30	31	

Sazaby Living Division　㈱ サザビー リビング事業本部

Furniture and household goods supplier / For promotional purposes
家具、雑貨輸入・製造・販売 / プロモーション　Japan　1993
BR: Sazaby's Furniture　D: Hatsuko Kobayashi / Chie Kusakari / Yukiko Yamazaki
size 255×255 mm

Kansai Paint 関西ペイント ㈱

Paint manufacturer / For promotional purposes　塗料メーカー / プロモーション　Japan　1993
CD: Tomoko Moriya　AD, D: Toshihiro Uchii　P: Hiro・Sanda　CW: Kazuko Eguchi　DF: Ships
size 520×360 mm

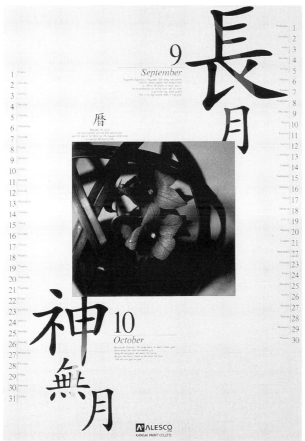

nature
1993

THROUGH THE NATURE

star
1

Sunday	Monday	Tuesday	Wednesday	Thursday	Friday	Saturday
·	·	·	·	·	1	2
3	4	5	6	7	8	9
10	11	12	13	14	15	16
17	18	19	20	21	22	23
24/31	25	26	27	28	29	30

earth

THROUGH THE NATURE

3

Sunday	Monday	Tuesday	Wednesday	Thursday	Friday	Saturday
·	1	2	3	4	5	6
7	8	9	10	11	12	13
14	15	16	17	18	19	20
21	22	23	24	25	26	27
28	29	30	31	·	·	·

sun

THROUGH THE NATURE

8

Sunday	Monday	Tuesday	Wednesday	Thursday	Friday	Saturday
1	2	3	4	5	6	7
8	9	10	11	12	13	14
15	16	17	18	19	20	21
22	23	24	25	26	27	28
29	30	31	·	·	·	·

Masaru Kawahara Inc.　㈱河原勝事務所

Graphic design firm / For promotional purposes　グラフィック デザイン / プロモーション
Japan 1993　AD, D: Masaru Kawahara　CW: Tomoko Ikenaga　size 590×420 mm

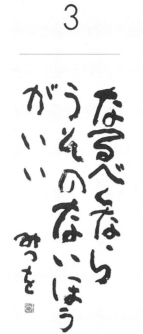

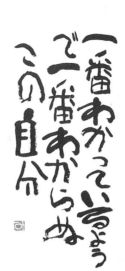

Nikon Sha Inc. ㈱而今社

Artist management / For retail sales　アーティスト管理 / 市販品
Japan　1994　AD, D: Takayuki Uchiyama　size 345×130 mm

Art Print Japan Co., Ltd. ㈱アートプリントジャパン

Stationery supplier / For retail sales
ポスター、カード製造・販売 / 市販品　Japan　1995
BR: graphic station　D: Noriko Kikuchi　size 350×100 mm

DESKTOP

JANUARY 1995

1 NEW YEAR'S DAY
SUNDAY

2
MONDAY

3
TUESDAY

4
WEDNESDAY

5
THURSDAY

6
FRIDAY

7
SATURDAY

DECEMBER 1994

FEBRUARY 1995

MAY 1995

28
SUNDAY

29 MEMORIAL DAY
MONDAY

30
TUESDAY

31
WEDNESDAY

APRIL 1995

JUNE 1995

In the dimension of difference, the Future is defined by Dreams.

DECEMBER 1995

31
SUNDAY

NOVEMBER 1995

JANUARY 1996

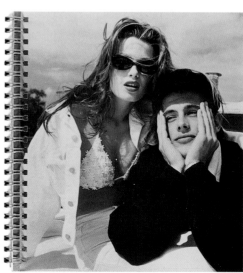

Guess?, Inc.

Apparel maker / For promotional purposes
アパレル メーカー / プロモーション　USA 1995　BR: Guess?
AD: Paul Marciano　D: Leslie Oki　P: Neil Kirk / Daniela Federici /
Dewey Nicks　CW: Emily Corey　DF: Guess?, Inc.
size 180×205 mm

Murai Optical Singapore Pte Ltd.

Eyewear retailer / For promotional purposes　眼鏡販売 / プロモーション　Singapore 1994
BR: Jean Paul Gaultier　CD: Shirley Chua　AD: Edmund Chia　D: John Phet
DF: OZ (International) Marketing & Advertising Pte Ltd.　size 220×158 mm

Millennium Japan ㈱ ミレニアム ジャパン

Apparel maker / For promotional purposes　アパレル メーカー / プロモーション　Japan　1995
BR: Trans Continents　AD: Hissashi Hamada　size 165×120 mm

Millennium Japan　㈱ ミレニアム ジャパン

Apparel maker / For promotional purposes　アパレル メーカー / プロモーション　Japan　1994
BR: Trans Continents　size 130×130 mm

Converter Adhesives & Chemicals Ltd.

Adhesives manufacturer / For promotional purposes　接着剤メーカー / プロモーション　India 1994
CD, CW: Shailendra Madan Kothari　AD: Naina Kothari　D: Quintessence Design Team
I: Prashant Sankhe　DF: Quintessence　size 160×210 mm

Gulliver Co., Ltd.　㈱ ガリバー

Printing company / For retail sales　印刷／市販品　Japan 1995
CD, DF: A Company Gulliver Book　D: Hiroko Murata / Kyoko Akatsuka　I: Shinichi Hoshi
size 140×135 mm

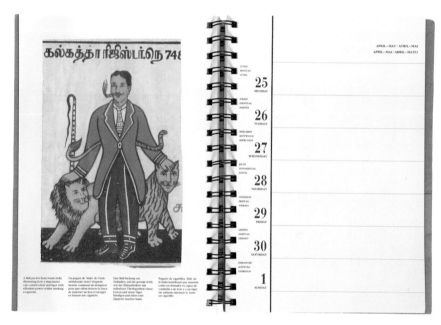

Redstone Press

Publisher / For retail sales　出版 / 市販品　England 1994
D: Julian Rothenstein　size 245×175 mm

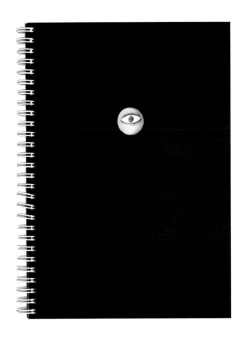

Corey & Company: Designers

Graphic design firm / For promotional purposes
グラフィック デザイン / プロモーション　USA　1994
CD, CW: Susan Gilzow　D, CW: Tammy Radmer
I: Mary Anne Lloyd　CW: Deborah Plunkett / Patricia O'hara
DF: Corey & Company: Designers　size 240×175 mm

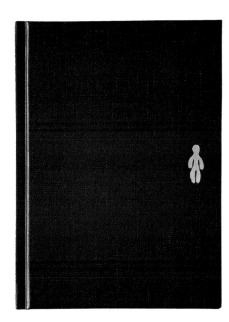

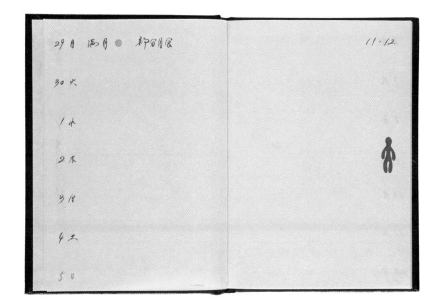

Jurgen Lehl　㈱ヨーガンレール

Apparel maker / For promotional purposes
アパレル メーカー / プロモーション　Japan　1994
D: Hideaki Matsuura　size 155×115 mm

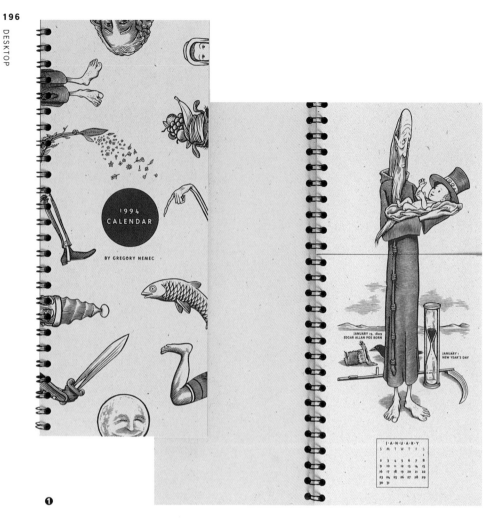

❶
Gregory Nemec

Illustrator / For promotional purposes　イラストレーション / プロモーション　USA　1994
D, I, CW: Gregory Nemec　size 226×95 mm

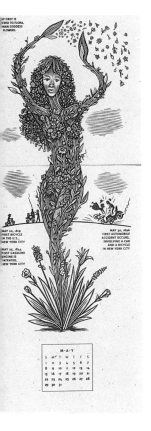

❷
The Manzano Day School

School / For promotional purposes　学校／プロモーション　USA 1994–1995
CD, AD, D: Steve Wedeen　I: Vivian Harder　CW: The Manzano Day School
DF: Vaughn Wedeen Creative　size 280×140 mm

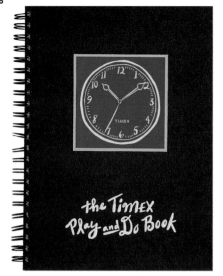

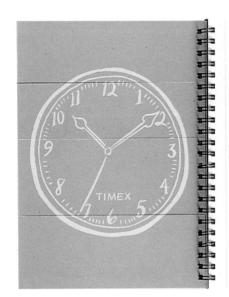

Timex Corporation

Watch manufacturer / For promotional purposes
腕時計メーカー / プロモーション　USA 1995
CD: Susie Watson　　CD, AD, D: Leslie Evans
AD, D: Cheri Bryant / Mary Brown　I: Mary Lynn Blasutta
DF: Leslie Evans Design Associates　size 147×203 mm

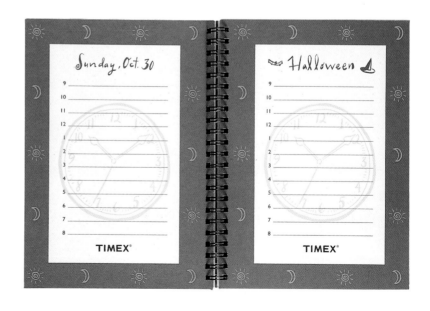

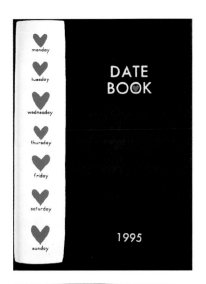

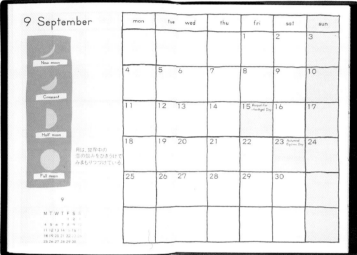

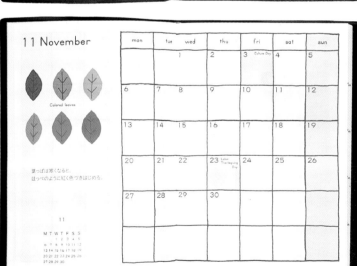

Æsop Co., Ltd. ㈱イソップ

Stationery supplier / For retail sales　雑貨、ステーショナリー製造・販売 / 市販品　Japan 1995
CD: Planning Dept., Æsop　size 150×110 mm

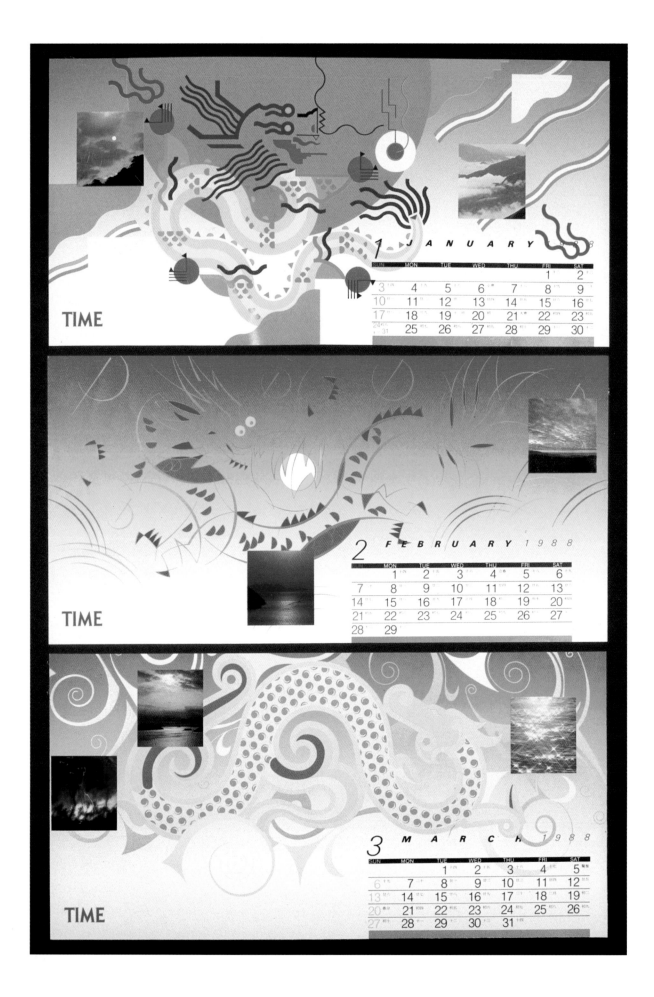

Time

Magazine publisher / For promotional purposes　雑誌出版／プロモーション　Hong Kong　1988
CD, AD: Hon Bing-Wah　D: So Man-Yee　DF: Kinggraphic Advertising & Production Ltd.
size 172×247 mm

National Travelers Life

Insurance company / For promotional purposes　生命保険 / プロモーション　USA 1993
CD, AD, D, I: John Sayles　DF: Sayles Graphic Design　size 110×180 mm

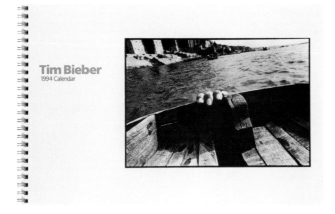

Tim Bieber

Photographer / For promotional purposes　フォトグラフィー／プロモーション　USA　1994
AD: Steve Liska　D: Marcos Chajez　P: Tim Bieber　DF: Liska and Associates, Inc.
size 215×330 mm

Body, Inc. ㈱ ボディ

Photographers / For retail sales　フォトグラフィー / 市販品　Japan　1995
AD, P: Takashi Shima　size 150×150 mm

January

February

June

September

Zoom Tokyo Office　㈱ ズーム東京オフィス

Graphic design & advertising / For promotional purposes　広告制作 / プロモーション　Japan 1994
CD, AD, D: Osamu Takeuchi　size 140×125 mm

Sazaby Inc. ㈱ サザビー

Furniture and household goods supplier / For promotional purposes
家具、雑貨輸入・製造・販売 / プロモーション　Japan 1990
D: Hiroki Kubota　I: Jessie Heatland　DF: Sazaby Design Center　size 190×190 mm

Sazaby Living Division ㈱ サザビー リビング事業本部

Furniture and household goods supplier / For promotional purposes
家具.雑貨輸入・製造・販売 / プロモーション　Japan　1995
BR: I.C.L. by Sazaby　D: Hatsuko Kobayashi　DF: Sazaby Graphic Design　size 65×65 mm

Umebara Design Office   梅原デザイン事務所

Packaging design / For private use   パッケージ デザイン / プライベート   Japan 1995
CD, AD, D: Shin Umebara   size 280×280 mm

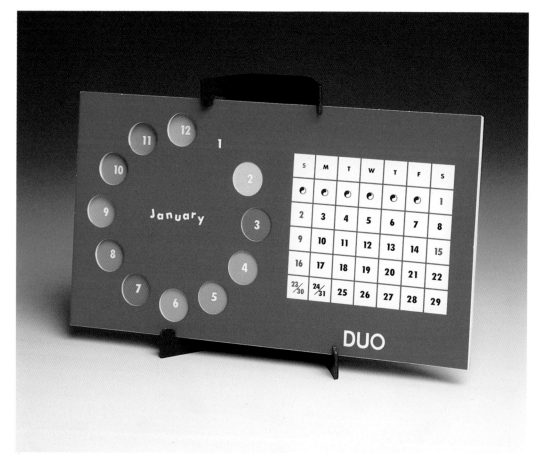

❶

❷

❶
DUO

Import car dealer / For promotional purposes   輸入車ディーラー / プロモーション   Japan 1994
CD: Makoto Nagata / Kozo Koshimizu   AD, D: Koji Toda   CW: Kozo Koshimizu   DF: C' Co., LTD.
size 110×200 mm

❷
DUO

Import car dealer / For promotional purposes   輸入車ディーラー / プロモーション   Japan 1995
CD: Chiemi amano   AD, D: Koji Toda   size 129×129 mm

Masako Fukiwake 吹訳 雅子

Illustrator / For retail sales　イラストレーション / 市販品　Japan　1994
D, I: Masako Fukiwake　size 90×90 mm

Art Print Japan Co., Ltd. ㈱アートプリントジャパン

Stationery supplier / For retail sales　ポスター、カード製作・販売 / 市販品　Japan 1995
BR: graphic station　D: Tomoko Yoshii　size 127×127 mm

NOMURA

JANUARY

SUN	MON	TUE	WED	THU	FRI	SAT
1	2	3	4	5	6	7
8	9	10	11	12	13	14
15	16	17	18	19	20	21
22	23	24	25	26	27	28
29	30	31				

MARCH

NOMURA

SUN	MON	TUE	WED	THU	FRI	SAT
			1	2	3	4
5	6	7	8	9	10	11
12	13	14	15	16	17	18
19	20	21	22	23	24	25
26	27	28	29	30	31	

NOMURA

SUN	MON	TUE	WED	THU	FRI	SAT
	1	2	3	4	5	6
7	8	9	10	11	12	13
14	15	16	17	18	19	20
21	22	23	24	25	26	27
28	29	30	31			

MAY

NOMURA

SUN	MON	TUE	WED	THU	FRI	SAT
			1	2	3	4
5	6	7	8	9	10	11
12	13	14	15	16	17	18
19	20	21	22	23	24	25
26	27	28	29	30		

NOVEMBER

The Nomura Securities Co., Ltd. 野村證券 ㈱

Securities firm / For promotional purposes 証券 / プロモーション Japan 1995
CD: Shinichi Enzaki / Kazuya Mototani AD: Kazuya Mototani D: Makoto Iida I: Lou Myers
size 147×147 mm

❶

❷

❶
Gallery Interform　ギャラリーインターフォーム

Stationery supplier / For retail sales　カード、カレンダー製造・販売 / 市販品　Japan　1994
CD: Masaya Yamaguchi　D, I: Sayuri Taniguchi　size 90×95 mm

❷
Æsop Co., Ltd.　㈱イソップ

Stationery supplier / For retail sales　雑貨、ステーショナリー製造・販売 / 市販品　Japan　1995
CD: Planning Dept., Æsop　D: Yumi Watanabe　size 130×100 mm

❶

❷

❶ **Ryu Ryu Co., Ltd.** ㈱ リュリュ

Stationery supplier / For retail sales　雑貨、ステーショナリー企画製作 / 市販品　Japan　1995
CD: Makoto Nishimaki　D: Hisanao Jyuma　size 232×165 mm

❷ **Super Planning Co., Ltd.** ㈱ スーパープランニング

Stationery supplier / For retail sales　雑貨、ステーショナリー企画製作 / 市販品　Japan　1995
BR: Mr. Friendly　CD: Takahisa Kamiya　size 180×108 mm

❶

❷

❶
Cubix Incorporated ㈱ キュービックス

Stationery supplier / For retail sales　ステーショナリー企画販売 / 市販品　Japan 1995
CD: Keita Kanazawa　AD: Toru Fukuda　D, I: Natsumi Tao　size 160×118 mm

❷
Cubix Incorporated ㈱ キュービックス

Stationery supplier / For retail sales　ステーショナリー企画販売 / 市販品　Japan 1995
CD: Keita Kanazawa　AD, D, I: Toru Fukuda　size 169×123 mm

❶

❷

❶
Cubix Incorporated ㈱ キュービックス

Stationery supplier / For retail sales　ステーショナリー企画販売 / 市販品　Japan　1994
CD: Keita Kanazawa　AD: Toru Fukuda　D, I: Teruko Arimoto　size 120×175 mm

❷
Æsop Co., Ltd. ㈱ イソップ

Stationery supplier / For retail sales　雑貨、ステーショナリー製造・販売 / 市販品　Japan　1994
CD: Planning Dept., Æsop　D: Sachiko Yanagisawa　size 210×210 mm

❶ Æsop Co., Ltd.　㈱イソップ

Stationery supplier / For retail sales
雑貨、ステーショナリー製造・販売 / 市販品　Japan 1995
CD: Planning Dept., Æsop　D: Tomoko Sakaime　size 200×160 mm

❷ Æsop Co., Ltd.　㈱イソップ

Stationery supplier / For retail sales
雑貨、ステーショナリー製造・販売 / 市販品　Japan 1994
CD: Planning Dept., Æsop　D: Akiko Obuchi　size 280×205 mm

❸ Æsop Co., Ltd.　㈱イソップ

Stationery supplier / For retail sales
雑貨、ステーショナリー製造・販売 / 市販品　Japan 1994
CD: Planning Dept., Æsop　D: Tomoko Sakaime　size 190×265 mm

Index

INDEX OF CLIENTS

INDEX OF SUBMITTORS

Calendar Collection

Jacket Design

Kazuo Abe

Art Director / Designer

Yutaka Ichimura

Editors

Ayako Aoyama

Mie Nakamura

Editorial Manager

Masato Ieshiro

Photographer

Kuniharu Fujimoto

Coordinator

Chizuko Gilmore (San Francisco)

English Translator & Adviser

Sue Herbert

Publisher

Shingo Miyoshi

2001年2月11日初版第1刷発行

発行所　ピエ・ブックス

〒170-0003　東京都豊島区駒込4-14-6-301

Tel: 03-3940-8302 Fax: 03-3576-7361

製版・印刷・製本　（株）サンニチ印刷

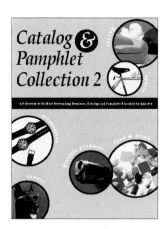

カタログ＆パンフレット・コレクション2
CATALOG AND PAMPHLET COLLECTION

個性的で斬新なデザイン展開で商品を効果的にプロモートするカタログ・パンフレット約250点収録。

This essential collection introduces more than 250 catalog and pamphlet masterpieces in 16 business categories, all designed for effective product promotion.

グラフィックビート：ソフトミックス vol.1
GRAPHIC BEAT THE SOFT MIX: vol.1

音楽シーンの先端ロンドン／トウキョウで活躍するデザイナー15人の作品約800点を紹介。

800 different designs spotlight the work of 15 designers at the forefront of the music scene in London and Tokyo.

グラフィックビート：ソフトミックス vol.2
GRAPHIC BEAT THE SOFT MIX: vol.2

音楽シーンの先端ロンドン／トウキョウで活躍するデザイナー14人の作品約800点を紹介。

800 different designs spotlight the work of 14 designers at the forefront of the music scene in London and Tokyo.

チラシ＆フライヤーコレクション
FLYER AND LEAFLET COLLECTION

街にあふれる様々なチラシ、リーフレット約500点をデザイン性で捉えた貴重な1冊。

This indispensable volume, presenting more than 500 flyers and leaflets, captures the very essence of design.

ブックデザインコレクション
BOOK DESIGN COLLECTION

国内外の書籍・雑誌の中から選りすぐった700冊のカバー・エディトリアルデザインを約1000カット紹介。

More than 1000 examples of publication design, from 700 books and magazines from all over the world.

レターヘッドコレクション
LETTERHEAD COLLECTION

レターヘッドを中心に、封筒、名刺、請求書など各種のビジネス書類を含むステーショナリー約250点を掲載。

Letterheads are in the spotlight here, but this collection also features envelopes, name cards, invoices, and other types of business stationery.

ワッペン・コレクション
FASHION INSIGNIA COLLECTION

120のファッション・ブランドの、お洒落でかわいいワッペン・エンブレムを約1000点紹介。

Over 3000 designs were scrutinized for this collection of 1000 outstanding emblems and embroidered motifs.

DM＆案内状コレクション
DM & ANNOUNCEMENT COLLECTION

世界中のクリエイターから寄せられた数多くの案内状の中から特に優れた作品約400点を厳選して掲載。

This issue includes 400 pieces of artwork, drawn from a vast number of submissions sent to us by creators from all over the world.

ヴィジブル ミュージック
VISIBLE MUSIC

デザイン、アイデアに優れた最新のCDジャケット約500点を、音楽ジャンル別に3つのカテゴリーに分けて紹介。

A collection of more than 500 CD jackets, all examples of the very best in contemporary design and creativity. Presented by genre and divided into three categories.

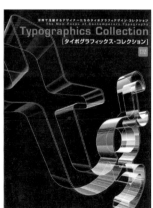

タイポグラフィックス・コレクション
TYPOGRAPHICS COLLECTION

世界で活躍するデザイナーたちのタイポグラフィーデザイン約350点を一挙掲載。

Over 350 superb typographic works by internationally-active designers compiled in a single volume.